The Ultimate
COMEBACK

Other books by Tommy Tenney

GOD CHASER series
The God Chasers
God's Favorite House
The God Catchers
God's Eye View
Prayers of a God Chaser
(Study guides and workbooks are available
for many of these books)

UNITY series
God's Dream Team
Answering God's Prayer
God's Secret to Greatness

COMPASSION series
Chasing God, Serving Man
Mary's Prayers and Martha's Recipes

FAMILY series
How to Be a God Chaser and a Kid Chaser
On Daddy's Shoulders

DEVOTIONAL BOOKS
The Daily Chase
Experiencing His Presence
Up Where You Belong

GIFT BOOKS
Heart of a God Chaser
God Chasers for Kids
God Chasers for Teens
You Are a God Chaser If . . .

OTHER BOOKS
Trust and Tragedy
Secret Sources of Power
Finding Favor With the King
Hadassah: One Night With the King
Hadassah: The Girl Who Became Queen Esther
One Night With the King
The Hadassah Covenant

The Ultimate COMEBACK

How to Turn a BAD NIGHT Into a GOOD DAY

TOMMY TENNEY

Faith Words

NEW YORK   BOSTON   NASHVILLE

FaithWords
Hachette Book Group USA
1271 Avenue of the Americas
New York, NY 10020

Visit our Web site at www.faithwords.com.

Book design by Fearn Cutler DeVicq

Printed in the United States of America

First Edition: January 2007
10 9 8 7 6 5 4 3 2 1

The FaithWords name and logo are trademarks of Hachette Book Group USA.

The Library of Congress Cataloging-in-Publication Data
Tenney, Tommy, 1956-
    The ultimate comeback : how to turn a bad night into a good day / Tommy Tenney. — 1st ed.
        p. cm.
    Summary: "An exploration how our disappointments are self-created by attaching our faith to the wrong things, and how faithful obedience can make spiritual restoration possible"—Provided by the publisher.
    ISBN-13: 978-0-446-57832-5
    ISBN-10: 0-446-57832-0
    1. Consolation. 2. Suffering—Religious aspects—Christianity. I. Title.
    BV4909.T46   2007
    248.8'6—dc22   2006007547

To those who proved you can comeback.
To Lisa, Marvin, and Jim.
To Randy, Mike, Charles, Dennis, J. D., Paul, and others like them.

Acknowledgments

A few lines on a page cannot acknowledge the depth of gratitude I owe to my host of teachers.

Some of them are ordinary men and women who did not even know they were teaching me as I observed them.

Others are extraordinary friends and fellow seekers.

To them I owe the deepest gratitude.

As "iron sharpens iron," our conversations challenged my thinking and birthed this book.

Special thanks to Jentzen Franklin, Phil Munsey, Perry Stone, and Edward Miller. And as usual, Larry Walker.

Contents

The Ultimate
COMEBACK

CHAPTER 1

You're Fired!

Have you ever had a bad day? You might have even had a bad week! Perhaps a bad month! Or heaven help us, a bad year! Some of those turbulent seasons of life begin with phrases such as:

"It's cancer."

"You're fired!"

"I want a divorce."

"With your record, no one is going to hire you."

"We've done all we can do . . . there is no hope . . ."

"If you can't make your payment, we will foreclose on your house."

"I hate you. I never want to talk to you again!"

Statements like these can unleash your worst fears at the very moment when you need your best faith! Ironically, it's when things are most hopeless that you most need hope. It's hard to summon up courage to face the future when you feel like a plant pulled up by the roots and laid out to dry.

If you are alive and breathing, at one time or another you will suffer loss or face a crushing crisis. Loss is a part of life, and it happens to all of us in some way or another.

Unjustified loss is even harder to handle! What do you do when life feels unfair? How can you respond and hope for restoration when dreams and aspirations have been ripped from your grasp?

Without getting into a lot of theology, let me assure you that bad news can knock on your door even when you are righteous before God. I'll give you just one name—Job.

> **What do you do when bad news has to wait in line just to talk to you?**

Bad news literally seemed to arrive so fast to Job that the messengers of doom had to wait in line at his door. Yet, through it all, Job handled himself in such a way that God praised and blessed him for it.

The biblical book named for him describes Job's long list of trouble, tragedy, and calamity and how he survived it all. Yet it begins with the simple announcement that Job "was blameless and upright, and one who feared God and shunned evil."[1]

That must mean that all of the calamities and sad events in Job's life weren't necessarily his fault—even if it looks that way. He was sailing through life as the world's richest man. He was blessed with a happy wife, a large family, and thriving livestock, land, and agricultural businesses. Things just seemed to be getting better and better every day. Then the bottom fell out of his life, and for no explainable reason.

Somehow, it would be easier to comprehend if we could pinpoint some secret sin or inherent character flaw in Job—then we'd know he *deserved* what he got.

Imagine that you were hired to lead a Fortune 500 company, earning a high six-figure salary with full benefits. Within twelve months business income was up 400 percent over the previous year, your company dominated its market, new products were being successfully launched, and even the unions loved you!

Your picture appears on the front covers of *Time*, *USA Today*, *Fortune* magazine, and *Christianity Today* (remember, you are a godly leader). All of the major TV talk shows want you to appear, and so do the leading late-night programs. The president is calling you weekly for advice on his upcoming national budget proposal.

You're Fired—No Reason Given

One moment you are at your desk on the ninetieth floor, then suddenly you are fired! No reason is given, but in only five minutes two security goons have thrown you onto a dirt pile on the sidewalk outside headquarters. All you have left is a torn yellow trash bag filled with a few broken family photo albums. Then things get *really* bad.

A courier walks over and looks down at your trash bag. Then, in disgust, he tosses a priority delivery package in your lap and walks away with an attitude.

The package holds a mixture of certified letters—all of them bringing more bad news: the IRS has impounded all of your vehicles, seized your house, and frozen all of your bank accounts and assets. The country club has canceled your charter membership, and is even billing you for the year's dues after your former company canceled its check for your membership.

While you are reading the contents of the tax indictment, an urgent messenger from the sheriff's department waits to talk to you. "We went to your residence to serve federal, state, and local subpoenas and criminal indictments," the deputy says. "And Mr. Job, we found all of your children dead. They were suddenly killed in a freak tornado while having dinner together."

Greeted by a Tearstained Face and a Menacing Glare

Dazed and dismayed, you drag your tattered trash bag to what used to be your home (remember, you lost the limo service, driver, and all your credit cards). There you find your wife waiting with a tearstained face and a menacing glare at the street curb outside your house, which is now enveloped in bright yellow police tape and bearing an IRS "Seized Property" sign.

"This is all *your* fault!" she snaps. "Why don't you just drop this religious stuff—what good has it done you? Just curse God and die . . . that's all you and your God are good for. And by the way—we're through, *loser!*"

Talk about a bad day! Job had to deal with his Mount Everest-like problems, and he somehow managed to trust God in faith, even when he didn't know why so many terrible things were happening to him.

How do you survive on those days when bad news has to wait in line just to talk to you? What do you do when your child says, "I hate you"? How do you get back on your feet after your spouse announces, "I just can't live with you any longer"? How do you resurrect hope when your doctor says, "I'm sorry, but there's *no* hope"?

Do you feel like Job? Does it seem as if it is always raining on your parade? There are answers to these situations.

Jesus remarked on circumstances like this when He said, "Rain falls on the just and the unjust."[2] He was not just talking about "showers of blessings" that make springtime flowers bloom and the world smell good. I think He was also referring to disastrous floods that threaten to sweep away the very foundations of our lives, not leaving the fragrance of flowers, but the stench of mold.

If bad news has clogged your in-box, you are obviously not alone.

The grace of the Bible is buttressed by the restoration of many people who have failed or suffered unjustly. But you may find it hard to imagine the incredible and virtually unbelievable biblical story of restoration that you are about to discover.

Imagine a president or prime minister hiring someone to be an intimate adviser, one who has direct access to him. Now imagine you've learned that this person's past crimes include a felony conviction for embezzlement, for illicitly siphoning off funds, for soliciting and receiving an under-the-table kickback? What if he had been wearing the uniform of his seven-year sentence as recently as the morning before he was hired?

How well rehabilitated would such a candidate have to be in order to be considered for employment in this age of political correctness?

To further darken the potential for this unlikely political come-back, what if this perpetrator had not merely embezzled from a government entity or corporation, *but from a charitable organization*—one known for significantly assisting needy families and entire nations in famine?

Even worse, what if this man took his under-the-table money while entrusted with the title of administrative officer, personal assistant to the president, and chief of staff for an internationally respected ministry?

This man didn't merely embezzle funds; he was found guilty of gross errors in judgment and breach of ethics. He boldly executed an embezzlement scheme in public and in broad daylight. He took so much that others had to *help him carry away* the fortune he embezzled—a historic gift to the *charitable organization* from a grateful high government official from a foreign nation!

Who could possibly believe there was a future for this convicted felon? Much less in any trusted high political or ministerial position?

In the heart of this book is just such a story. While you may not have made such highly publicized mistakes as these, none of us would want our private shortcomings made public. All of us need restoration from our mistakes and missteps in life, whether they are great or small, public or private.

When reaching for your restoration, your "declaration" should be, "If God has done it for them, He can do it for me!"

How Do You Come Back from This?

Virtually every hero and heroine in literature and the Bible had to persevere through tough times. We often encounter the same type of situations each of them faced. The question haunts our minds: *Will I survive, much less thrive?*

I know at least one man who probably felt like you do. Lazarus, a man known as the friend of Jesus, died prematurely before Jesus could reach him. How do you "come back" from death? Perhaps that is how you feel. All hope is lost, the door is closed, locked, and they threw away the key. What happens next? His story can be your story too! Can hopelessness be turned into hope?

All hope seemed lost until Jesus called Lazarus out of the grave. Friends and loved ones shouted, "He is alive!" But something is *still* wrong with the picture.

Lazarus had "survived" his trial by death—somehow he found himself standing outside the tomb. The tomb of death had become the womb of life, but he was *still* bound in his grave clothes as if his destination were still in doubt. Would he merely survive, or would he thrive?

Sometimes you can survive a crisis only to live forever in the "limbo land" of the unrestored. Perhaps a mistake you made or an unjust decision someone else made put your dreams, plans, and hopes in the grave. How do you not only survive the crisis but truly come back?

Everyone there knew those outer trappings of death and darkness had to go. One eyewitness testified that the previously deceased man "*came out* bound hand and foot."[3] (Most of us do.)

He may have been breathing again, and we may assume Lazarus could see a dim glow of daylight and hear the muffled tones of human voices once again through his macabre bindings, but he was still separated from life by the remnants of death. Freedom of movement, communication, and any opportunity to feel the comforting touch of others were out of the question.

I wonder, *Did Lazarus fear he might slip back into death's darkness if someone didn't set him totally free?*

Jesus called in a loud voice, "Lazarus, *come out*!"[4]

Turn Around and Come Out!

He is *still* saying that. He's standing outside the dead-end doorway of loss and He's saying, "Turn around and *come out*! Come *back*! Come *back* to life!"

Even after Lazarus "came back," even after he turned around and came out of the door of death, the door no one exits—the door of a tomb—he was still bound.

Sometimes, even after salvation has visited your life, frustration still binds you. Things are not "back" like they used to be. You feel as if your hands are tied and your feet are bound.

Are you ready to do *more* than merely exist? Lazarus was alive, but he wasn't really living. He was existing! Jesus said, "I have come that they may have life, and that they may have it more abundantly."[5]

Notice the placement of the comma: "I have come that they may have life—*COMMA*—and that they may have it more abundantly."

Perhaps you are living on the wrong side of the comma. Life before the comma—that's mere existence. The abundant life exists on the other side of the comma. The life where not only are you breathing, but loosed, unbound, set free, and back in your living room visiting with your sisters, Mary and Martha. Restored!

Have you noticed that Jesus looked at the circle of friends who gathered around the tomb of Lazarus that day and said, "*You* loose him, and let him go."

> **Don't let your past hold your future hostage.**

One of the most beautiful acts of restoration is when others realize what God has done, and they take the last remnants of the grave clothes off you. You are then not just forgiven by God, but forgiven by your friends. It is at this point you realize that your past no longer holds your future hostage.

They unwrapped Lazarus. Blessed be the "Unwrappers"! Purpose in your life that you will be one of those who unwrap the grave clothes of past failures from people.

When Lazarus was finally freed from the trappings and remnants of death by his friends, he left the rags of failure at the opening of the tomb and returned to his house to find it filled with food and gifts left for his grieving family. The food at home for a mourning family was turned into a feast for celebration! Now that's a picture of restoration!

Lazarus should be your hero, your "poster boy"! If he can "come out" of the tomb, then you can "come back" from your failures.

Can you imagine how Lazarus felt as he struggled to sit up in the tomb? He wriggles his feet to the floor, and attempts to maintain his balance for a moment before tottering and wobbling through the door of the tomb with his feet and hands still bound!

It was probably difficult to accomplish. But Lazarus purposed in his mind, "I'm coming out!" You must do the same!

We recognize and revere heroes because they did not quit, they clawed their way back. That's why they are our "heroes." Tough times are the womb of heroes, and failure is often the womb of success.

Even if their own mistakes precipitated their personal disaster, somehow they found a way to "come back," to initiate a magnificent "turnaround"!

I'm old enough now to know that my view of heroes is not just those who conquered and never failed, but also those who "came back" from the abyss of failure. A recent reading of heaven's hall of heroes in Hebrews 11 emphasized that fact to me.

> And what more shall I say? For the time would fail me to tell of Gideon and Barak and Samson and Jephthah, also of David and Samuel and the prophets: who through faith subdued kingdoms, worked righteousness, obtained promises, stopped the mouths of lions . . .[6]

It is amazing that among the names of those who are called heroes of faith, Samson's name is included. It is also inspiring!

This listing is not just of those who never fell and never failed, but the purposeful inclusion of one of the Bible's great failures and incredible comebacks appears here. Heaven made sure Samson's name was included to give all of us hope. Despite his moral failure with Delilah, he made "the list"!

Why else would such a "failure" show up in the Bible's "Faith Hall of Fame"? It seems there is hope for us "normal" people who often seem to fail as much as succeed.

Sometimes bad things happen to you "just because"—you do nothing to cause them or deserve them. But often our suffering can be traced directly to our own wrong decisions, wrong motives, selfish desires, or foolish choices. That is the natural outcome.

One of the "laws of physics" states that "for every action there's an equal and opposite reaction." One **Everybody needs restoration.** could restate this in the light of the biblical law of sowing and reaping as, "Whatever a man sows, that he will also reap."[7]

Your fall may not be as spectacular as Samson's, but we can agree that everybody makes mistakes and has failures. Ergo, *everybody needs restoration*. It doesn't matter whether the need is physical, spiritual, relational, mental, or financial.

If it's broken, it needs to be fixed.

If it's missing, lost, or stolen, it needs to be replaced.

If it is tainted, scattered, or battered, it needs to be restored.

Perhaps what you need is a restoration road map. At some point, hope must be restored and inspiration renewed—whether from a decade-long sentence as in Samson's case,[8] or from a days-long detour from the path of righteousness and purpose.

How long did Samson wait to make the one good decision that reversed his course in blindness? The one that caused his name to be dusted off, shined back up, and stuck on the display shelf with the rest of the Hall of Famers?

As you read these words, perhaps you are experiencing a reverie of memories. Life's road takes a lot of twists and turns. It is fast one moment, and slow the next; complete with unexpected hairpin curves and exhilarating acceleration down straightaway stretches.

Then there are those times when life comes to a complete standstill, a dead halt. You reach a "dead" end.

A bad decision at a previous fork in the road forces you to put your life in reverse. Then begins the inch-by-inch retreat in backward motion, the grinding revisit to a place where you can make your course correction and return to the proper path. God does allow U-turns.

If you happen to glance again at God's Hall of Fame in the Book of Hebrews, you will find our unlikely hero, Samson, inserted a mere two words away from Gideon, interspersed just before David and Samuel. If *his* name can show up there, then your name can show up also.

Samson's story can become your story! A tale of remarkable restoration!

CHAPTER 2

The Tale of the Almond Tree
My Future Looks Bright . . .

One time several years ago, my youngest daughter insisted on buy-
ing a twig-like lemon tree growing in a small plastic container. As
usual, she prevailed and the purchase was made. As a dutiful father, I
made sure to place the scrawny little tree in the sunshine. She hoped
we would soon enjoy some tart lemons from our new investment.
That first week, she checked the little lemon tree daily to see if she
could make lemonade.

Four or five years went by before that tree ever produced any
lemons. One day she excitedly ran in to announce: "Daddy—there is
a lemon growing on our lemon tree!"

When it was finally ready, that tree produced a bumper crop of
fruit! We actually had to prop up the finger-thick limbs on the little
tree because of all the lemons hanging on them. The next year we had
no lemons! In fact, I haven't been able to coax even one lemon from
that tree since! That one lemon tree is about the extent of my
orchard-tending experience!

But, I once read a story about a crisis in the life of a tree from the
orchard of a master arborist. It may not sound like much, but one
part of that story just rocked my world. *Let me rehearse the tale to you . . .*

Once upon a time there was a little almond tree. Although it
started off as a little twig of a sapling, the master of the orchard

carefully worked the soil around it, and made sure it was watered and lovingly cared for.

The little almond tree struggled and pressed through every obstacle to grow as tall as possible. The progress continued more and more each week as the master tilled the soil around the tree. Everything seemed to be going very well.

The little almond tree said to itself, "I am going to be the best almond tree in the orchard for my master. I am going to produce the best fruit." The thought of failure never even crossed the little tree's mind. All it could think of was, *I will be the best!*

Typically, fruit trees don't produce fruit quickly. It takes time to wring moisture out of the soil, to put down deep roots, and to grow strong limbs to support heavy fruit.

In fact, it often takes years for almond trees to produce their first fruit, but the little tree was trying its best to hurry along the natural process. That little tree wanted more than anything to squeeze out a blossom and make it produce some fruit for the master.

Unfortunately, the young tree just didn't understand that in its immaturity, it did not have the root structure to gather up enough nutrients from the soil. It could not transfer enough moisture to the branches to produce blossoms and fruit yet.

Roots Go Long and Deep for Hidden Sources

Every drop of moisture in a tree and in its fruit must be squeezed from the soil by its roots. Those roots grow long and go deep to tap hidden sources of water and nourishment below the surface. Molecule by molecule the roots wrestle water from the earth. As the sap rises through the trunk of the young tree, fresh layers of new growth join the old and the tree continues to grow in girth and maturity.

It seemed as though it would take forever, but every so often the master came by to check around the roots and trunk of the tree. Occasionally he would pull weeds that intruded on the tree's space and add nutrients to the soil.

The little almond tree stretched himself tall and straight, thinking,

I am taller than all the other young trees around me! Yes, I am definitely going to be the best. With high hopes, the little tree continued to grow.

Everything seemed to be fine. The little tree finally reached the maturity of a sapling, still easily bent but growing straight and tall. "Perhaps this year," the almond sapling told itself. "Perhaps this is the year for me, when the warm spring sunlight begins to energize my buds, stems, and leaves. Once the early sap begins to rise through the branches, things will begin to happen. Maybe this year I will produce fruit."

It was a special year. One day the master came by, and he seemed particularly interested in the little almond tree this year. But he didn't follow the annual spring routine. He didn't perform all of the usual once-yearly cleanup tasks.

Normally, to ensure there was plenty of water around the roots, he would craft some kind of earthen retention dike to retain water during the rain; but on this early spring day, he didn't do that.

This time, the master circled the tree, giving it a really close perusal. Then he reached out with both hands to grasp the tree's young trunk. When the master gently bent the tree trunk a little bit, the almond tree said to itself, "Oh, he's checking my root system. Maybe that is why he bent me a little." *O-o-o—that hurts!* thought the little tree.

Cut Off at the Root!

With the little tree bent and holding its breath, one hand of the master firmly encircled the bent sapling. With one swift movement he reached for his ax and cut off the tree at the root!

In shock, the little almond tree thought, *What did I do? I did the best I knew how. I'm sorry I didn't produce the fruit that you thought was necessary.*

The little almond tree actually felt betrayed! The very one who seemed to take such care and interest in him was now the one who separated the almond tree from the source of its nutrients. He couldn't believe the master himself had cut him away from his roots. How would he survive? What had he done wrong?

As if it wasn't enough to separate the almond tree from its source of life-sustaining nutrients, the master meticulously moved from branch to branch bending each one. Then he broke them off! Whenever he came across a branch that was too big to be broken, he cut it away with his ax.

The seemingly brutal process continued until the almond tree was stripped bare of leaves and branches! At that point, the beautiful young tree had been reduced to nothing but a chopped-off tree trunk, the kind he had seen thrown into the fire!

The almond tree just couldn't understand it. *How am I supposed to bear fruit? All I ever wanted to do was to be the best almond tree I could be. Now I have no more branches. Will I be thrown into the fire with the other discarded branches?*

All the almond tree could think about was how he used to be. *How long will it take me to grow more branches?* Then the tree remembered something it overheard one day about "grafting."

Hope rose again with the thought, *Oh, maybe that is what the master is going to do. Perhaps he plans to "graft" me into a stronger root system somewhere.*

Then the master began to carefully peel away the bark from the almond tree trunk.

I Don't Understand What's Going On

The bark is the outer covering that protects the inner heart of the tree itself. It also preserves the moisture levels inside the tree and transports nutrients throughout its full height. Under normal circumstances, the bark helps the tree remain a living organism, allowing it to grow and not dry out. The bark of a tree is its only protection. Now the master himself had begun stripping away the bark. The little tree felt naked and exposed.

As it lay there stripped and uprooted, the little almond tree wrestled with an unending string of unanswered questions summed up in one thought: *I don't understand what's going on.*

Finally, the bare almond sapling was laid in the hot sun. Each day, when the master returned, the almond tree thought to itself, *Maybe he is going to graft me in now.*

But instead of grafting the tree into another root, the master simply turned the almond tree a half turn, allowing the hot sun to hit the other side of the bare tree. With each day that passed, the heat of the sun pulled more and more moisture out of the very heart of the almond tree. The strong voice of hope had dimmed to a whimpering whisper.

The master turned the sapling a little every day to make sure it dried straight and true. The slow drying process took many days, and only when every hint of moisture had been drawn from the almond tree did the master finally return and say, "Okay, now I think you are ready."

Submitted to the Pain of an Aborted Dream

Then the master picked up the dried-out sapling and began to walk while leaning on its sturdy length. A startling revelation suddenly dawned on the almond tree: *"I'm no longer an almond tree! I am a staff. I'm a rod. So that is what the master wanted—he wanted to turn me into a walking staff, a strong rod to lean upon.*

"Okay, I can accept that. I will be the best staff and the strongest rod ever made. I will support his weight and I will not break. I will always be there for him. I'm going to make him glad he picked me."

The little almond tree submitted itself to the pain of its aborted dream. It decided, *"If I can't be what I thought I was going to be, then maybe I just didn't know what I was supposed to be. I am going to be the best staff that any tree could ever be."*

It was painful to experience the process of my life being uprooted. Suddenly and unexpectedly, I was cut off from the very things from which I drew my nutrients, the source of my life. Then my protection, my shield against the elements and dangers of the outside world, was stripped away. Now I am left alone. Yet, no one else is as close to the master as I am. I am literally in his hand; I am strength to him. When he is tired, I am there . . . the best staff he could ever find.

Some length of time went by—perhaps it was a matter of weeks, or months, or even years. The rod that used to be an almond tree was faithful, and it always remained within the reach of the master.

The master and rod were separated only when the master carefully leaned the almond rod by the door of a tent before entering. Each time when he left, the master was careful to pick up his rod again.

When the path grew steep and treacherous, when the master's feet began to slip or falter . . . "Thy rod, thy staff, they comfort me."[1]

Rising Tensions and Outright Complaints

So the almond tree became a comfort to his master, and he quietly reconciled himself to face the facts of his new role, even though it seemed starkly different from his dream of what he thought he would be.

Amid rumors of rising tensions and outright complaints, the top leaders of the community were called into a serious meeting—and the master of the almond rod was summoned.

The almond rod was often carried to such meetings, so that wasn't uncommon. The almond rod never really understood what was being discussed. The leaders talked on a higher level about greater things than he understood. The almond rod only knew he must be strong and try to do the best he could.

Something happened during *this* meeting, however, that was different from any other meeting the almond rod had seen.

When the chief leader stood to make an announcement in a firm voice, twelve men suddenly rose to their feet. One of them was his master. Then suddenly, everything changed once again.

Some of the men sent servants scurrying out of the meeting tent, while others hurriedly searched through piles of belongings neatly stacked around the perimeter of the tent.

The master called for no servants. Instead, he walked directly to the opening at the front of the tent and removed the almond rod from the place where he leaned it against the tent.

The master then did the unthinkable! As if the rod hadn't been cut enough, the master pulled a knife from the folds of his robe and began gouging gashes into the strong dry wood. Blowing away the particles of wood and nodding in approval, he mouthed his readiness.

Now everyone knew who had done this to the little almond tree; the master had branded his own name onto his staff.

The Master Threw Down the Almond Rod

He solemnly returned to the center of the meeting area and stood in place as if anchored to the ground with stakes. Slowly he scanned the faces of the men crowded into the meeting tent.

When all twelve men had finally assembled in a circle with their rods in hand, the master threw down the almond rod in the very center of the meeting tent, where all could see it. As if on signal, the rest of the men did the same with their rods.

Fear flooded the thoughts of the almond rod. He'd seen the same thing happen to other pieces of wood. First they had been carefully laid together in a bundle, and the next thing he knew, someone had ignited the pile of dry wood with a burning ember or coal!

Each time he saw this happen, the hungry flames of the fire quickly consumed every piece of wood in the stack. That was the last thing he wanted to happen to him.

He knew that his master would need heat from a fire some day, but he never believed it would be at *his* expense. Now he was beginning to question every action and decision.

In a panic, he told himself, *Anyone will tell you that when you pile wood in this fashion, it becomes fuel for the fire!*

The little almond rod grew even more frightened when the master turned on his heel and walked away, followed by the other men in the circle.

Utter silence fell on the crowd of leaders, as the almond rod lay on the ground with other rods stacked on top of and beside him.

Then the strange old man who was the chief leader with a commanding presence picked up the almond rod along with all of the others and carried them away.

Another More Mysterious Place

The old man carried the rods into a dark room and carefully parted the thick folds of a heavy embroidered tapestry dividing the room they were in from another darker, more mysterious place.

Thrusting his hands through the linen curtain embroidered with cherubim in hues of blue, purple, and scarlet, the man roughly threw the twelve sticks into the thick darkness. Without a word, the man turned and walked away. The thick folds of the curtain instantly closed once again, leaving the little almond rod and the rest of the rods alone in unsettling silence, and near absolute darkness.

Absolutely abandoned. Every dream crushed, every hope gone, the almond rod felt alone and desperate in a dark place. *All I ever wanted to do was be the best almond tree I could be. When that didn't happen, all I wanted to do was be the best staff I could be. Now it seems as though these men have decided to get rid of the lot of us.*

> And the LORD spake unto Moses, saying,
>
> Speak unto the children of Israel, and take of every one of them a rod according to the house of their fathers, of all their princes according to the house of their fathers' twelve rods: write thou every man's name upon his rod.
>
> And thou shalt *write Aaron's name upon the rod of Levi*: for one rod shall be for the head of the house of their fathers.
>
> And thou shalt *lay them up* in the tabernacle of the congregation before the testimony, where I will meet with you.[2]

Have You Ever Been "Laid Up"?

In many parts of the United States, it is common to say of someone confined to a hospital bed, "They are going to be 'laid up' for a good two months, as a result of that accident." One command appeared to change destiny's course for the almond rod, and it came without warning or option: ". . . Lay them up in the tabernacle of the congregation before the testimony, where I will meet with you."[3]

The almond rod didn't have a choice about when, how, where, or what would happen. Forces above and beyond the almond rod's control or influence dictated the act, the time, the place, the method, and its purpose.

The almond rod's journey appeared to end with a question mark, not an exclamation mark. Often, a shepherd's staff will have a crook bent in the end of it—turning what had been a straight sapling into a *question mark*. A question mark is often an exclamation mark that got bent at the end. Life itself is filled with both exclamation marks and question marks.

> *The almond rod's journey appeared to end with a question mark, not an exclamation mark.*

If you were to step back and look at the rod, you would notice that the straight part of the rod closely resembles the top portion of an exclamation mark. If you look at the top of the rod, you might notice that the crook—the curved or bent part at the top—looks very much like the top portion of a question mark.

When you seek direction or instruction from the Great Shepherd, the only way to discern which "end" of His rod you follow is by being still and waiting in the presence of the Lord.

Everything that "could have been" or "should have been" was reduced to empty "what if?" speculations and imaginations. No parties or celebrations were scheduled for the almond rod's future. All future possibilities had collapsed into the gloomy reality of the present, a dark day of devastation, despair, hopelessness, and abandonment.

Have you ever felt this way? Do you know what it is like to feel stripped, bare, vulnerable, and powerless?

The almond rod's dreams had been dashed and permanently frustrated. This marvelous genetic wonder of an almond tree could never produce the fruit prized around the world for its delicate aroma and sweet taste. He had been abruptly severed from what he once believed was his greatest purpose and destiny.

From the perspective of the young almond tree, he had been cut off and diverted another direction before his time. Have you felt this way?

Beware of the "Until" Clause

"Plan A," according to the almond tree, just never included the possibility that he would one day be turned into a lifeless staff or rod. Nevertheless, the almond rod adjusted to "Plan B." His abrupt and unasked for change of life and purpose.

Everything seemed to go along just fine and without incident *until* . . .

Most of us can easily relate to the "*until*" clause. How many times has life actually seemed to be looking good for you "*until* . . ."?

For the almond-tree-turned-leader's-staff, life was finally beginning to look good again, *until* he found himself suddenly gathered up and thrown into a pile; like just another discarded stick of wood consigned to the fire.

Did I just describe some aspect of *your* life?

- Was it your marriage we were talking about?
- Was it your twenty-year career, flushed down the drain labeled "corporate downsizing"? And just as it looked like a promotion was headed your way?
- Was it the fifteen-minute doctor's appointment that just robbed you of thirty-five years of life with a mere three-word sentence, "You have cancer"?
- Is the piercing pain of betrayal still searing your emotions and memories years after the agonizing act?
- Was it the forfeiture of all the benefits of your college education, social standing, and family memories over a momentary indiscretion or ethical compromise?
- Do you feel as if you have been cut off at the roots by bitter divorce or an unjust judicial decree?

Are you still trying to comfort yourself with the words "I was only doing the best I knew how to do"?

Perhaps you never claimed to be the "best," or to be the "biggest" tree in the orchard. You never claimed to be the most productive employee, but you *were* doing the best you knew how to do. You gave it your all, only to discover in surprise that your best didn't seem to be good enough.

"It hurts to think the Master Himself separated me from the very thing that He called me to do." Is that what you are really thinking? Do you want to tell Him in heart-baring honesty, "God, I thought You put me here! Why are You now separating me from my obvious destiny?"

Many people want to experience the *"ultimate turnaround"* and the *"greatest comeback"* in history, but without having graduated from the school of the *"ultimate underdog."*

Perhaps you've never had to battle your way past adversity. You've never had to hold your chin up when the world was trying to press your head down. Honestly, if you've never been in that place, then perhaps this book isn't for you.

But if you thought you'd never make it back, if you were sure that you'd never survive—much less thrive—perhaps you feel that the place of the *underdog*, the *underappreciated*, and the *underachiever* has become your permanent place in life. You may even realize that because of wrong choices you've made, this is where you "ended" up.

You feel like failure is a common friend. Even the biblical record reminds us of our propensity to fall. "For all have sinned, and fallen short of the glory of God . . ."[4]

You may feel as if you will never again see the light of day. Are you ready for the rest of the story, for the "latter end" of the matter? I can give you a hint of hope: *"I know a way out . . ."*

CHAPTER 3

I Feel Stripped, Bare, and Dry
Is There a Way Back?

When we last viewed the young almond tree . . .

Every dream had been crushed; every hope felt gone. The almond rod felt absolutely abandoned, desperate, and confused in nearly absolute darkness behind the thick drawn curtains.

If the almond tree's story described your life, and if that sad moment in lonely isolation resembled the end of your story, then I would mourn with you. However, the fact that you are still here and are still reading this book tells me your story is not finished.

In the memorable phrase coined by commentator Paul Harvey, "Now it is time for the rest of the story." Just because you are behind the curtains, that does not mean the opera is over! It's time for a curtain call!

Sometime during the longest and loneliest night of its existence, the little almond rod began to feel something strangely familiar flow through its cells. It had been so long since he had that feeling he didn't even know what it was. It seemed impossible and beyond belief.

Moisture was seeping through the withered rod that used to be a tree. How could this be? This almond tree was merely a stripped and dried-out rod with no roots to draw moisture from the earth. For a long time, it had been detached from everything that could or would provide sustenance or nutrients.

Nevertheless, the almond rod felt life-giving moisture surging through him!

> Just because you are behind the curtains, that does not mean the opera is over! It's time for a curtain call!

The next thing he knew, the almond rod felt a "swelling" where there used to be only dried and shriveled cells. In the dimness, he even felt the odd sensation of skin or bark stretching. *How is that possible? All of my bark was stripped away long ago!*

Surely it was only a dream . . . it had been so long since anything like this had happened, the almond rod didn't know whether to rejoice or be afraid.

A faint blue glow seemed to illuminate the room, and it was enough for the almond rod to witness an impossible miracle . . . he literally saw a bud burst into view from his side! Then another bud exploded from its smooth surface on the other side. While a third bud emerged in yet another place, the first bud actually began to blossom . . . in the absence of sunlight or living roots planted in sustaining soil.

Fruitful and Dumbfounded in the Presence

Then the second bud blossomed, followed by a third and a fourth. On and on it continued, all night long! Then, to the amazement of the dumbfounded almond rod, one of the blossoms miraculously produced an almond fruit that ripened on the spot! This was not supposed to happen! This had never happened!

All of this happened at the very place and time that the almond tree felt most abandoned and broken. What happened in that lonely place and why?

> And thou shalt lay them [the twelve rods] up in the tabernacle of the congregation before the testimony [the Ark of the Covenant], *where I will meet with you.*[1]
>
> And Moses *laid up the rods before the LORD in the tabernacle of witness.*

> And it came to pass, that on the morrow Moses
> went into the tabernacle of witness; and, behold, *the
> rod of Aaron for the house of Levi was budded, and brought
> forth buds, and bloomed blossoms, and yielded almonds.*[2]

Notice that God told Moses to lay up the rods in the Most Holy Place right in front of the Ark of the Covenant "*. . . where I will meet with you.*"

Supernatural Habitation Trumps Dark Desperation

When Moses laid the dead and discouraged rod of Aaron in the near darkness of the Most Holy Place, the almond tree was alarmed. He thought, *Why would my master abandon me in what seems to be a lifeless place of punishment or disposal for unwanted things?*

Here is where we, along with the almond tree, begin to understand, "When my dreams are dying, His plans are often just beginning."

In reality, the lifeless almond rod was about to discover a secret of God's presence—*one night in God's presence and you can become what you always dreamed you were supposed to be.* God does His best work in the secret place.

> *One night in God's presence and you can become what you always dreamed you were supposed to be.*

The almond rod didn't understand or fully realize that he was *still* an almond tree until the following morning. All of the dreams and the genetic disposition he originally possessed had somehow been resurrected. He was still alive and flourishing. But he didn't understand how or why!

Even though the almond rod was totally "disconnected" from soil and sun, he felt a strange glow and warmth of life flowing through his dried-up cells. This feeling didn't resemble anything he had ever received from the soil, and the sun never provided anything as potent as this!

Something greater, deeper, and more ancient than sunlight or soil was at work here. The normal action of chlorophyll and all of the

When my dreams are dying, His plans are often just beginning.

scientifically categorized laws of nature that usually affect the growth of almond trees had been suspended. It had never really happened like this before.

Under the best of circumstances, it normally takes much time for a healthy almond tree to produce buds, blossoms, and ripe almonds! But this process didn't take place over a period of days, weeks, months, or years of interaction with soil, water, and light. It happened between sundown and sunrise!

The little almond tree became everything he ever wanted to be in about twelve hours! And it all happened while the almond rod was "laid up" *in the presence of God.*

This is a simple story. Has it reminded you of times in your life when you felt disconnected from what matters most to you?

One night in God's presence can accelerate your destiny!

Have you ever struggled to understand why God apparently picked you up, stripped you bare, and plopped you outside your comfort zone? Do you wonder why He would leave you feeling stripped?

I'm Drying Up!

Have you been telling yourself (and anyone else who will listen), "I'm drying up! Something is missing and I *have* to be reconnected. I need to get into the soil; I need to get back to the stuff that used to make me happy"?

Be careful. It is so easy to become connected to the "farm." It really isn't about the "farm," it's about the "Farmer." Life isn't about the soil of our earthly existence or even the rays of the sun. It is all about *God's presence.*

One night in God's presence can accelerate your destiny!

If a day is "as a thousand years, and a thousand years as one day,"[3] then do you understand that God can take a thousand years' worth of blessing and infuse it into your life *in only one day? Remember the miracle of the almond rod.*

I don't know how long you've suffered with the fear that your life was drying up, feeling cut off from your destiny. Life can leave you feeling as if you have been stacked up like firewood, just waiting for the painful oblivion of the flames.

Even during those moments when you feel as if you have been shoved into a dim place and abandoned, His presence is there. Perhaps you don't understand your present circumstances; take comfort in the promises of the "Farmer"! God knows where you are.

His Presence Resurrects the Disconnected

If you *wait* on the Lord, even when you feel "laid up" in dim isolation, you will gain new strength.[4] Life will spring up again. Things will happen in a short span of time that seem beyond explanation or understanding. His presence reconnects the disconnected! Things will happen even while you appear to be disconnected from all of your natural sources of life and strength.

If you can persevere through your season of being "laid up" or "laid off" on earth, then Paul said there is "laid up" for you a crown of righteousness![5]

> *He imparts His life when you lay down your life—in His presence.*

People will look at you and say:

- "How did that fruit come from your life? You aren't even connected the right way!"
- "You aren't touching the 'soil' of the politically correct 'inner circle.'"
- "You don't have any money and your company is only a year old—how did you get that contract?"
- "Nobody predicted you would do this well—you just don't have the credentials or experience for this! The rain didn't come into your life—but here you are blooming and producing fruit!"

Only one answer will do for you (and for your critics). *It is time to lay everything down in the presence of God.* Only an intimate encounter with His presence can resurrect your dreams and restore you to the destiny for which you were born.

It doesn't matter to God whether you failed or others failed you. You may have suffered injustice yesterday or fifty years ago. He imparts *His* life when you lay down *your* life—in His presence.

"But I don't see that happening for me! I haven't seen things moving that way in my life. I still can't feel a thing."

He May Do Everything in Just One Night!

Perhaps your path will follow that of the almond rod. It may be that God will not restore your life piece by piece. He may do everything in just one night. He may choose to resurrect your dead dreams in one powerful moment of intimacy! Remember this: Never underestimate the potential of one encounter with God's presence!

"But you don't know how stripped I feel."

May I plumb the depths of your deepest need? It is not about getting and keeping the right job. It's not about being in the right location or marrying just the right person. It is not about making sure that you've positioned yourself to get the most spotlight exposure in front of the most important people. It is not about "dressing for success" or "posing for promotion" in the corporate culture.

> *Never underestimate the potential of one encounter with God's presence!*

Just do this—*make sure that you are in God's presence.* Learn what the almond tree learned, *the soil is not your true source.*

The laws of nature, the principles of business, the protocols of politics and personal gain; they may all try to stake their claims on your life:

- "Sink your roots in the soil of the land."
- "Plant your feet firmly on the rock of financial investment and prudent business principles."
- "Put yourself in the driver's seat—remember that you are Number One."

God's Approval Outshines All Others'

People may tell you, "You cannot grow unless you have the light of the sun, the approval of the higher powers, shining on you." The truth is that only One Power matters; the favor and approval of God outshines all others'.

Perhaps you feel forgotten, as if you were left on a shelf or stuffed in the

> **The soil is not your true source.**

closet of forgetfulness. "What bothers me the most is that I feel as if *God* did it to me. And I was just doing my best." Sometimes we resent the very circumstances God has sent to develop us.

You may even feel frustrated with authors, preachers, and the testimonies of other people trumpeting God's faithfulness. Perhaps you are thinking:

> *I just want to make it through this month! I don't need all that stuff, I just need to understand what You are doing, God. Those people are in the limelight, but I am in the shadows on a back shelf somewhere. I'm stripped and naked, and without a prayer. I don't even have a branch to produce or hold any fruit. I have nothing.*

The little almond tree seemed to have nothing either—once it was stripped of root, leaf, limb, and bark, it had no sunlight, no soil, and no access to the nutrients essential to life. It had to feel abandoned and alone. Yet it shared one thing in common with *you*, and that missing factor is the Eternal Wild Card nearly everyone overlooks—it found itself in *the presence of God.*
Again, never forget this one thing: One night in the presence of God can accelerate your destiny.

> **Sometimes we resent the very circumstances God has sent to develop us.**

"I don't see any movement in my life. How can anyone say my dreams are coming true?" *Just stay in His presence.*

Don't Move Me—My Life Is in this Presence!

After that night in the presence of the Lord, Moses returned to pick up the rods. Aaron's almond rod had budded, blossomed, and produced ripe almonds. This twelve-hour wonder was so incredible that you could almost imagine the little almond tree asking Moses that morning, "Please don't move me away from here. *My life* is in this presence!" But the miracle must be displayed.

The little rod that budded was shown to the mass of people that gathered. This was his "moment in the sun"! Oohs and aahs thundered. He had never been so admired, or approved. But the little rod now felt uncomfortable in the glare of the sun. Normally this would be the perfect environment.

Never fall in love with the spotlight. Never fall in love with the crowds. As amazing as it sounds, the little tree now longed to be placed behind the veil.

There in that thick and private Presence, he was hidden from the crowd. He was spared the test of pride in an accomplishment he could not claim or explain. Never take credit for what you cannot duplicate. He longed to be hidden in the very Presence that had transformed him from a dead token to a living sign and wonder. The little almond tree now felt more at home in the secret place than the public place.

Then something even more amazing occurred. As a testimony to the grumblers, doubters, and disbelievers in the crowd, God had Moses return the little almond tree to its place right in the box called the "Testimony" or the Ark of the Covenant, with the mercy seat on top. This was where the glory of God hovered day and night, representing the *visible presence of the invisible God.*

> Then Moses brought out all the rods from before the Lord to all the children of Israel; and they looked, and each man took his rod.
> And the Lord said to Moses, *"Bring Aaron's rod back before the Testimony*, to be kept as a sign . . ."[6]

The presence of God was the true source of life and power that brought life to the dead almond tree, *not merely the box or the tent where He chose to dwell.* It's not about the "farm" where you are placed; it's about the "Farmer" who places you.

The Lord wanted to make the *same point* to the Israelites, and He wants you and me to understand it also. I believe that as long as the little almond tree stayed in God's presence, it still had green leaves, blossoms, and almond fruit.

"How can you say that?"

I say it on firm theological footing because I am in agreement with the writer of the Book of Hebrews, who said:

> . . . [the Tabernacle] which had the golden censer and the ark of the covenant overlaid on all sides with gold, in which were the golden pot that had the manna, Aaron's rod that budded, and the tablets of the covenant.[7]

Everything in His Presence Lives

The manna that God provided for the Israelites in the wilderness would not keep overnight by divine design. When the rule was broken, maggots infested the manna and it began to stink.[8]

However, the manna Aaron placed in the Ark of the Covenant stayed permanently fresh and alive, because it was to be a *visible witness* to the provision of God to generations who knew nothing about the forty-year wilderness journey. It was also a testimony to the power of God's presence and a prophetic picture of the Immanuel—*God with Us*—the Bread of Heaven who would come.

> And Moses said to Aaron, "Take a pot and put an omer of manna in it, and *lay it up before the LORD, to be kept for your generations.*"
>
> As the LORD commanded Moses, so Aaron laid it up before the Testimony, *to be kept.*[9]

Did you notice those words, "to be kept"? That is not an accidental phrase. It literally means "the presence of God stands guard like a sentry to insure preservation!"[10]

Supernatural Life Flows from His Presence

God wasn't interested in future generations seeing shriveled up, wormy, or rancid samples of ruined manna. He commanded Moses and Aaron to place the manna and Aaron's almond rod *in His presence* where life would continually flow and supernaturally preserve them "to be kept." Nothing stinks and nothing dies in His presence.

Your fragile dreams will stay permanently fresh in the presence of God! Unfortunately, one of our strongest human tendencies is to lean on all the things *we can do* rather than on what *He has already done.*

"I've got to run. I've got to put myself in the right soil! I need to be at the right job. I need to do this, I need to do that."

No, you need to learn the value of the presence of God. When everyone around you assures you that your dreams won't come true, press into His presence and stay there until life returns. Freshness is a by-product of intimacy, whether in a marriage or in worship.

You too may have been stripped of all protection and life-giving resources. You may feel as if every bit of moisture has been sucked out of your life, as if you are disconnected from anything that could give you energy to go on. That is where you tap the presence of God and discover its power. When all seems lost, *find yourself in the presence of God.*

The genesis of your restoration is an encounter with the presence of God. The maintenance of your restoration is connected to continued exposure to the presence of God.

Avoid Rigid Man-Made Rituals and Mechanical Mantras

Let me warn you that our discussion about God's presence is *more than mere words* or *rigid man-made ritual.* Don't expect to lean on some mechanical mantra of deeper Christian experience, thinking in it you will find the secret of God. People have made this mistake for untold generations. It is not about an equation or fleshly formula—it's about relationship.

In the apostle Paul's day, people who should have known better mistook the act of "invoking the name of Jesus" for the reality of actually *knowing* Jesus. They had no relationship with Jesus.

Seven sons of one of Israel's highest-ranking religious leaders fancied themselves to be ancient versions of "ghost busters" and demon exorcists.

> Then some of the itinerant Jewish exorcists took it upon themselves to call the name of the Lord Jesus over those who had evil spirits, saying, "We exorcise you by the Jesus whom Paul preaches."
>
> Also there were seven sons of Sceva, a Jewish chief priest, who did so.
>
> And the evil spirit answered and said, "Jesus I know, and Paul I know; but who are you?"
>
> Then the man in whom the evil spirit was leaped on them, overpowered them, and prevailed against them, so that they fled out of that house naked and wounded.
>
> This became known both to all Jews and Greeks dwelling in Ephesus; and fear fell on them all, and the name of the Lord Jesus was magnified.[11]

The name of Jesus isn't some magical equation—there is a presence attached to it. You cannot disconnect the Lord's presence from His name and expect that name to retain restorative powers. It is powerless to invoke the name of Jesus to do the will of man.

Just for a moment, disconnect the term "presence" from the word "God." Perhaps we will learn more about the word "presence" by applying it on the simpler level of the natural realm.

When Dad comes home from a trip, how do the kids react—especially when they are young? (Mine are so old now that they yawn and say, "Oh, Dad's home.")

My oldest daughter is now married. Her husband has children from a previous marriage—two little girls, ages three and five. Overnight I became a "step"-granddad. (*I am in love—these little girls have stolen my heart!*)

I forgot the overjoyed excitement that *little girls* can bring to a house. (They will be with me next Friday night. I am so distracted I can hardly write!)

These two little girls are often around our house now, so when I enter the front door I have to prepare. "Oh, PawPaw Tommy is here!" Once I step through the door, they run toward me at breakneck speed (how I love to hear the pitter-pat of those little feet), and simply launch themselves as human love missiles into the air!

If this has ever happened to you, then you know that you have to be braced and ready. Little children will just jump right into your arms whether you are ready or not.

It's all because my *presence* came. Not just because they are at Paw-Paw Tommy's house, but because PawPaw Tommy is here!

There are times when the presence of a dad does something nothing else can do. If there has been trouble or crisis in my family while I was away, my wife will just grab me when I come home and say, "I just feel better knowing you're here." Evidently, there is something about my presence that seems to say, "Everything is going to be okay."

When we say "the presence of God," we often want to put stained glass and steeples over the image in our minds. Perhaps it makes us feel better on a different level.

No, I want you to connect the presence of God with the presence of a loved one or perhaps the presence of a baby. *The very fact that they are there* brings joy, lightens your heart, brightens your day, and makes your burdens seem lighter.

Being in God's presence answers questions before you can even ask them. Learn to retreat into His presence. "The name of the LORD is a strong tower; the righteous run to it and are safe."[12]

Don't you just feel safe when you are in the presence of your heavenly Father? How do you stay there?

Do you know that *worship is the art of "hanging out" with God*? Please pardon my slang, but it helps refresh our view of something so easily taken for granted. It is very simple: *The almond tree stayed fresh by just being in the right place.*

There simply is no bad way or wrong way for my kids to tell me, "I love you, Dad." Too often we fall into the rut of thinking there is such a thing as "bad" worship or "wrong" worship. The only qualifications I can think of are those Jesus gave us—to worship the Father "in spirit and in truth."[13] Worship is how you act in the presence of God. Prayer is the language you speak when worshipping.

> **Worship is the art of "hanging out" with God.**

When we talk about worship, we often insist on adding recommended or required body positions, music styles, clothing guidelines, class curriculums, and countless other rules and regulations.

Can you imagine what the disciples were thinking when they were surrounded by an angry crowd and the father of a demonized son who complained to Jesus, "Your disciples tried to cast the demons out *and they couldn't!*"?[14]

This incident triggers a mental picture of all the different ways the disciples tried to pray for this boy.

- I wonder if some of the men in that era believed in the "two-handed chiropractic prayer" so popular today? This is where maximum effect comes only when the victim's head is bent back until the neck cracks. (Did I say "victim"?)
- Then there were the "disciples of the softer touch," the ones who believed the most spiritual prayer method was to lightly touch the person.
- Perhaps the majority belonged to the Capernaum Oilers, who favored the liberal application of oil on the forehead using the "sign of the cross with the index finger" technique.

- Is it possible that some of the disciples prayed standing on one foot while others prayed energetically with both feet firmly planted (and without oil)?

Prayer isn't a matter of mechanics; it is a matter of understanding.

When you invoke the name of Jesus, do not use it like some "abracadabra" magic equation or manipulative incantation taken from a child's cartoon or an occultist text. When you invoke His name, you are calling for His presence. And that's that.

When my wife calls my name throughout the house, or when she calls me on my cell phone, she is doing *more* than merely using my name. She is calling for my *presence*. She isn't interested in merely hearing my voice on a recording, or in seeing my picture pasted on a life-sized stand-up poster. She wants *me!*

Do You Want His Benefits or His Presence?

When you invoke the name of Jesus, you connect His presence with that precious name. If you love His presence, you will act differently toward Him than if all you really want are the benefits connected to His name.

You don't really love Him if all you want to do is steal God's credit card, to prostitute the name of Jesus, to line your pockets or protect your future. You just love His stuff and the seemingly unlimited bank account that comes with it.

We take marriage vows that promise faithfulness "in sickness and in health." Honestly, you don't know what love is until you've been through some tough times. Sometimes, real love hurts.

I once sent some flowers and a note to my wife that said, "To someone who is as easy to *stay* in love with as she was to *fall* in love with."

I can say that because I remember the time when we had only been married two or three years. Doctors said I was suffering from a brain tumor and I spent thirty days in the hospital, completely incoherent. My young wife slept on a hard, unpadded cot right beside my bed. That was over twenty-five years ago.

Love isn't *true* love until somebody has walked with you through some tough times. Love isn't the recitation of rehearsed vows or a passionate kiss on a red carpet. Sometimes love shows up best through unconditional commitment that says, "I like hanging out with you. In fact, I would rather hang out with you in a hospital room than with anybody else in a banquet hall!" Love is a tough curriculum in the "University of Life."

From Darkest Hour to Brightest Moment in His Presence

God's presence can transform your darkest hour into your brightest moment.

Some people can barely tolerate God, even when the choir is singing and sunlight is streaming through stained-glass windows. They look at their watches, crease their church bulletin, and say, "Okay, let's hurry up and get through this. Let's get through the sermon and to lunch on time." They seem to not enjoy being in God's presence.

Most of these folks are good people who consider themselves to be good Christians, but I have some real questions about this attitude. *How is it that we say we want to go to heaven and spend an eternity doing what we don't appear to enjoy doing for even an hour on earth?*

God's presence rarely hovers where "Christian fast-lane worship" is preferred. I am trying to say this as diplomatically as possible, but the Bible says worship will be our main activity and chief joy in heaven. Do you know why? Worship is the art of knowing how to be in God's presence. Its fruit is the joy of just being there.

Some people are so distracted that they never realize it when God's presence invades a room or meeting. They are so spiritually rude that they never acknowledge Him and can hardly wait to get rid of Him so things will return to their miserable version of "normal."

It is possible to get so caught up in having church that we fail to acknowledge that He is present in our meetings! Have you ever been to a party where the hosts were more interested in making sure the party was set up just right than in meeting, greeting, and enjoying the people who were there? We are all prone to these kinds of things.

Worship is the only part of our services that God gets anything out of! If you are worried about heresy at this point, take a deep breath and read on. I don't mind being quoted, but just don't misquote me.

Too many good people adopt a bad attitude that says, "I can be late for church. Yes, I may miss the worship, *but I'll be there for the Word.*"

What we are really saying is: "I may miss God's part, but I'll be there for *my part.*"

God does not learn one thing from our preaching. In fact, God has *never* gained a single new "revelation" or "reminder" from any-one's teaching—and that includes the best messages of Billy Graham, Charles Spurgeon, Martin Luther, Peter, John, or Paul the Apostle.

Worship is the only part of our services that God gets anything out of!

No human being has ever or will ever teach God anything. We are incapable of helping God or of talking Him into doing anything. Can you imagine God nudging Michael or Gabriel and saying, *"Can you hand Me a pen or quill? I want to write that down—I didn't know that!"*

"Okay then, why do we even bother to teach and preach?"

The purpose of preaching and teaching is to raise up worshippers. It is to equip us for the work of the ministry, not merely provide work for the ministers. Even the Westminster Catechism speaks of the duty of man to worship and enjoy God.[15]

I'm not trying to merely teach you how to say little magical equations "in the name of Jesus." If you say His name and *disconnect* His name from His presence, then it's just another name. The restoration of the almond rod that budded was directly connected to the presence of God, not the name of the tent.

Your restoration is connected to your worship.

What does all of this have to do with "I feel stripped, bare, and dry"? The almond branch was resurrected and revived by the presence of God. You are never "stripped, *or* bare, *or* dry" when you are clothed by God's presence.

When we find our path cut off and our lives out of place, *the "comeback" is easy to talk about, but the "way back" is sometimes hard to find.*

Worship and prayer from the midst of trouble can usher you into His presence, and it is precisely in His presence where you find the starting point for the "way back." Yes, *there is a way back!*

There were other people named Jesus during the Lord's earthly ministry. Jesus—Yeshua or Jehoshua—was not an uncommon name in that day. If you say His name, and you disconnect His name from His person, you are merely saying ordinary words without supernatural effect.[16]

When you say the name of Jesus and you have a *relationship* with Him, you invoke the very *presence* of the Lord into the situation!

> The "comeback" is easy to talk about, but the "way back" is sometimes hard to find.

Only God's presence can transform life's greatest failures into our greatest triumphs.

There is power in the presence of God. And that, my friend, is where the process of restoration begins.

CHAPTER 4

The "Oops" Chapter of Life
What Happens When You Trip Over Your Own Feet

Have you ever said something and wished you could grab those words and cram them back in your mouth? Have you walked into a room and *instantly* realized, "Oops, I've gotta get out of here!" and you tried to back out and close the door—knowing it was too late? One error in judgment, one bad decision, and life as you know it is over.

Have you ever done something that you wished you could undo? This is when a mother's adage, "You can't 'unspill' spilled milk," is an unwelcome phrase.

Have you ever known someone who was close to greatness, but never seemed to achieve it? Do you know people who worked for greatness—great people, great causes, great institutions—but never became great themselves?

Let me tell you the story of just such a man. He was so close to fame when he entered the "oops" chapter of his life that he ranks as one of the Bible's greatest disappointments.

His story remained behind the scenes for most of his life; he always seemed to be the invisible "bit player" whose role was easily overlooked and forgotten. He never quite showed up on the stage as a headliner.

We focus on this little-known figure because the best way to make right turns in our lives often is to retrace the mistakes, wrong turns, and failures of others in the past.

This man had real potential as a superstar, a "gold standard" model for victorious living in his day. Given the opportunity to finish well, his story might have possessed the qualities of a heroic biography. Most of his adult life, his career path quietly modeled that of his boss, the prophet Elisha, who in his quest for a double-mantle anointing, had once held the same position of assistant for his predecessor Elijah.

This man reminds me more of the mailroom clerk who might live two doors down in a nice apartment complex. In his early days, he was as politely invisible as an auto parts salesman, a cable guy, or a medical transcriptionist laboring faithfully in her home office. You get the feeling life wouldn't be quite as comfortable or efficient without them, but you can't say that you know or remember their names most of the time.

Call this man a "professional gofer" or personal assistant to the president of the company if you wish. He was also the one who showed up with coffee, the ever-present briefcase, and the business papers the president accidentally left at home. In the final analysis, he was *close* to authority but never quite in charge.

This man was the one who scheduled all the appointments, who would meet and greet visitors, and who could have always kept a fresh pack of moist disposable paper towels ready to wash the eccentric prophet's hands. That's the role he played, an assistant prophet.

As the story begins, there seems good reason to believe that the star of our story would one day take Elisha's place as chief prophet. (That was the pattern—the senior prophet would select a protégé from among many applicants and train him "on the job.")

Irony amplifies the folly of this man's "oops tripping episode" because he obviously was the heir-apparent, the next in line to the office of the prophet. He was only one step removed from greatness, and now it appeared it was his turn.

This man's troubles began after he second-guessed the leader he served. Some people may be tempted to make excuses for him and say, "All the guy did was what was normally done but at a different time," but in reality he committed a gross error of presumption.

He acted on the unspoken assumption that he was exempt from the usual standards of the common man because he served a great leader and national hero. As a result, he was cursed, literally! He was blacklisted in the worst possible way.

His name was Gehazi.

He Needed Restoration—and Was Least Likely to Receive It

If anyone ever needed restoration, this was the man—and because of the sentence of judgment pronounced over him, he seemed the least likely of all men to receive it.

To truly understand the depth of Gehazi's fall, you must hear a parallel story of Naaman's rise to restoration. These men from two different nations encountered each other in a miraculous series of events centered upon the prophet Elisha, but once Gehazi and Naaman parted ways they headed in dramatically different directions.

One hit bottom and began his climb back. The other fell from the dizzying heights of potential and carried his family with him in his descent to the abyss.

Naaman wasn't just an ordinary man. He was the chief of staff, the secretary of defense, and the top military strategist of the nation of Syria. He was the country's number one military general, the leader who could accomplish the impossible through sheer force of will and overpowering skill as a military leader.

His story is also one of the most amazing accounts of restoration that I've ever seen in the Scriptures, but it is best known by the unusual catalyst for recovery that it contains.

All of us love to hear stories of restoration, but we want to avoid the story of the crises that created the need for restoration. We want to fast-forward the DVD or hurry up the story, saying, "Skip all the boring stuff—tell me about how things get good." We forget (or choose to ignore the fact) that something has to die or wither before it can be restored.

Skip "That Dying Part" of the Story

The painful part of the story is often buried at the bottom of our social topics list. It reminds me of a fictitious interview CNN landed with Lazarus in the Holy Land. The reporter asked, "Lazarus, what does it feel like to be raised from the dead?" (We can listen to that part of the story over and over again.)

I can see Lazarus brushing aside a smelly leftover strand of burial cloth that strayed into his face as he answered, "Being raised from the dead, that was pretty cool. *But that 'dying' part* . . . now, that was tough!"

Before you can honestly talk about restoration, you must be willing to personally identify with how bad a problem can get. (Are you prepared to squirm a little and open up the tomb with me?)

Let me warn you that some of the things you are about to read will seem so implausible and impossible that you will think to yourself, *You made that up!* If I don't show you chapter and verse in the Scriptures, you just might think you are reading a really wild fiction book. Once again, where God's Word is concerned, fact is definitely stranger than fiction. The tomb of failure can become the womb of success.

The tomb of failure can become the womb of success.

In the fifth chapter of Second Kings in the Old Testament, we discover that famous military leader I mentioned. Naaman was a foreign army general who was "on top of the world" but at the same time was trapped in the grip of an incurable, infectious, and fatal disease.

> Now Naaman, commander of the army of the king of Syria, was a great and honorable man in the eyes of his master, because by him the LORD had given victory to Syria. He was also a mighty man of valor, *but a leper.*[1]

Ruined by a Three-Word Footnote

The Bible says this Syrian war hero was the head of the army for the king of Syria, and that he was "great and honorable" and "a mighty man of valor." Then it ruined everything with a three-word footnote: ". . . but a leper."

Even the mighty can be brought down by seemingly insignificant and unseen things. Perhaps somebody carrying the microscopic seeds of leprosy sneezed in the vicinity of General Naaman during one of his victorious military campaigns. Perhaps it was even an early version of biological warfare—no one but God really knows.

Leprosy is almost nonexistent in the developed nations of the Western Hemisphere today. The last time I checked, I believe that only one leprosy hospital was still operating in the United States—and it was in the process of closing down. The last few people who lived there no longer needed to live in isolation due to great advances in medical knowledge and treatment options.

Imagine a New Nightmare Disease . . .

The only way you and I can begin to understand the impact of leprosy on people in Naaman's day is to think of cancer as a *highly contagious* disease (think "common cold"), and roll it together with the social stigma and terminal prognosis of HIV/AIDS.

What if every time you visited a loved one sick with a deadly and contagious combination of cancer and HIV/AIDS, you risked catching it yourself? Would you visit often? Think of all those with cancer; now ask yourself, "What if it was contagious?"

How often would you visit someone sick with cancer? How afraid would you be? How lovely would they be?[2]

If you contracted leprosy and you loved your family, you would never again hug them, touch them, or draw close to them. Your infectious plague would qualify you for immediate and permanent expulsion from your home, your neighborhood, your church, and, in most cases, your own city! Once labeled a leper, then for the rest of your earthly days you must also shout, "Unclean! Unclean!" to warn away normal people anytime you are near the public.

This new fictitious nightmare disease we've imagined finally allows us to understand the fearful and paralyzing impact of biblical leprosy.

When leprosy struck Naaman, I think perhaps he thought to himself, *It would have been better to die in battle than to discover I am cursed with this!* The disease often first appeared as a little scaly place on the forehead or, typically, on the back of the hand. Perhaps it was after Naaman was checked by his army doctor in Syria that his life hit absolute bottom.

Disease and sorrow are equal opportunity destroyers. It doesn't matter how high a person climbs on the professional, social, or political ladder. No matter how powerful, well-connected, or wealthy you may be, bad things can crop up in your life. Tears can stain silk pillowcases just as easily as threadbare cotton pillow covers. It doesn't matter.

Can you see the mighty General Naaman, Syrian commander in chief, walking home from the doctor's appointment? He probably didn't even want to walk onto his own property. His little girl sees him from a distance and shouts to everyone else in the house, "Daddy's home, Daddy's home!"

As a caring and compassionate father, he probably sent word ahead of his arrival on that day. When his little girl wanted to run out the gate to greet her daddy as she usually did, the head servant urgently commanded the other servants, "No, no, hold her. Stop her! Don't let her go out there. She doesn't understand."

The little girl was confused, and she cried out to her mother, who stood weeping just inside the front door of the house, "Mommy, why won't they let me go hug Daddy? Why can't I . . . ?"

I Won't Be Coming Home Anymore

Perhaps Naaman was weeping, and when his wife started to walk toward him despite his previous warnings, he quickly said, "Don't come any closer—I am unclean. I just came by the house to tell you good-bye. I won't be coming home anymore." Then he began to tell the full story behind the bad news.

Between uncontrollable bouts of weeping and sobbing, he gives the instructions that will remove him from their lives forever: "I need you to pack up my stuff. And by the way, have the servants burn the furniture in our bedroom. There is money set aside to replace what you need. Don't worry about a king-sized bed this time . . ."

It is likely that some of General Naaman's servants contracted the same disease that he had, and in the same way. (Since slaves were viewed as property, it really wouldn't have mattered in that culture if some servants were deliberately exposed to leprosy to further advance Syria's military success and top leader.) No doubt they had been exposed.

The Bible states that General Naaman heard a rumor from a maid, an Israelite servant girl originally captured during Syrian military campaigns against Israel. Perhaps she was helping Mrs. Naaman pack up the general's things. Seeing the mistress of the house weeping over Naaman, who had left the house forever, the little Israelite slave girl made a simple statement:

> If only my master [Naaman] were with the prophet who is in Samaria! For he would heal him of his leprosy.[3]

Will You Allow Bitterness to Affect Your Destiny?

The compassion of this slave, this young girl from Israel, just amazes me. She refused to allow the bitterness of slavery to eat into her soul. I suspect that most people in similar circumstances would be tempted to curse their captors in their bitterness.

"I hope they all get leprosy. May it spread death, pain, and sorrow to every one of them! It's only what they deserve. They separated me from my family, they carried me captive into a foreign land by force, and now I have to take care of the very people who stole my life! I wish upon them all of the pain they've given me and more!"

The young Israelite maid demonstrated the truth we all must

learn: If bitterness does not affect your spirit, then it cannot affect your destiny.

Some people let their souls get contaminated along the way. They let the poison of bitterness invade their spirit. Choose the higher path. Make your decision and declare, "It doesn't matter what my circumstances are, I will not allow bitterness in my spirit." Learn to navigate the rough waters of "downturns" while avoiding the rocks of bitterness.

> **If bitterness does not affect your spirit, then it cannot affect your destiny.**

That is the beauty of the story of the almond rod. The almond rod said, "I may not be a tree, but I'll be a rod. Whatever happens, I will not let it affect my spirit."

Don't allow circumstances to affect your spirit. Take control over your thought life. If you open the door for bitter or discontented thoughts, they will just roll over and over in your mind. Stop the pity parade now!

Circumstances Will Not Dictate My Level of Worship!

At some point you just have to say, "That's it. I refuse to let circumstances dictate my level of worship! If Paul and Silas can worship in a jail cell, then I can worship in this adverse circumstance."

Mrs. Naaman didn't waste any time passing along to her husband the news from her servant girl. In the very next verse, General Naaman the leper tells the king of Syria about the Israelite prophet who could cure leprosy. The king, eager to take care of his star player, wasted no time. He loaded up his general with a fortune in gold, silver, and exotic clothing, and sent him directly to Israel along with his personal letter of introduction.[4]

The Israelite king was suspicious of anything Syrian (and for good reason!). His first reaction was to get angry because, in his mind, the Syrian king's letter required him to heal the leper himself! If and when he failed to do so, he believed the Syrian king hoped to pick a fight with him. He was so upset that he tore his clothes in anger and frustration.

Elisha the prophet heard about the king's fit of anger and sent a messenger to ask, "Why are you tearing up your clothes? Send the guy to me . . . and the King of Syria will know there is a prophet in Israel."[5]

> Then Naaman went with his horses and chariot, and
> he stood at the door of Elisha's house.[6]

When we read "horses and chariot," we think of an archaic and quaint mode of travel seen in history books and movies. We need to get a fresh mental picture of Bible events to really understand their impact. Only VIPs rode in chariots.

He Rode in the Latest Model Rolls-Royce Chariot

When Naaman pulled up in front of Elisha's house, perhaps he was riding in the latest model Rolls-Royce chariot, accompanied by a whole retinue of military aides and servants. A complete caravan followed him loaded with gold, silver, and fine clothing and garments fit for a king. He had a letter of recommendation from one king and a map drawn by another. Nothing like this had *ever* been seen in that area—much less pulling up at the preacher's house!

Now General Naaman, the conqueror of nations and ruler of armies, was used to receiving the red-carpet treatment wherever he went. People bowed their heads when he showed up or walked by. Why? Everyone knew this Syrian commander in chief had the power to cut off any heads that did *not* bow.

Everybody took care of Naaman because of who he was, and where he had come from. But when he pulled up in front of Elisha's house, the prophet didn't even bother to come out!

Go Jump in the River!

Instead, Elisha the prophet sent Naaman a message through a servant (probably his butler and personal assistant, Gehazi):

> And Elisha sent a messenger to him, saying, "Go and
> wash in the Jordan seven times, and your flesh shall
> be restored to you, and you shall be clean."[7]

This is what happened according to my own personal "translation" of Elisha's message through Gehazi to Naaman (with tongue held firmly in cheek):

> I'm not going out there, and I'm not going to lay
> hands on him. Tell Naaman I said, *"Go jump in the
> river! Seven times!"*

Just imagine how the mighty General Naaman answered that message. "I beg your pardon?! Just who does this preacher think he is? I'd like to meet this guy *in person!* I can't believe this. Does he really understand who I am?"

> But Naaman became furious, and went away and said,
> "Indeed, I said to myself, 'He will surely come out to
> me, and stand and call on the name of the LORD his
> God, and wave his hand over the place, and heal the
> leprosy.'
> "Are not the Abanah and the Pharpar, the rivers of
> Damascus, better than all the waters of Israel? Could
> I not wash in them and be clean?" So he turned and
> went away in a rage.[8]

This Syrian MIG (Most Important General) was bent out of shape. In a furious rage, the most powerful military leader in the Middle East put the pedal to the metal and burned rubber on his Rolls-Royce chariot as he and his entourage tore out of the prophet's driveway.

This insult could have international consequences. Representatives of the Syrian and Israelite media corps scrambled for juicy sound bites, and military strategists on both sides began pulling out old battle plans for an impending battle royal.

"I expected a lot more from this so-called prophet," Naaman must have said to himself. "That pompous preacher wouldn't even step out of his office long enough to see me! The king of Israel trembled and the prophet won't even speak to me directly."

Looking for Quivering Hands and Magical Incantations

At the very least Naaman expected to get "the Moses treatment," with the dramatic raising of the arms and the outstretched prophet's staff. Then maybe the prophet would extend his quivering hands over Naaman's leprous body and utter magical incantations.

"But no, this preacher had to be a wise guy!" Naaman said to himself. "He actually told me to jump in the sorriest excuse for a river I've ever seen. This Jordan River isn't a river at all—it's a meandering creek that is too muddy to drink and too filthy for bathing! It is just *another* insult heaped on top of the others!"

Some people today do the same thing Naaman did thousands of years ago. They would rather just *keep* their problem and leave with their dignity intact than lose their dignity and solve their problem! "I want my healing, and I want it my way."

Sometimes God sets up a barrier of obedience for you to surmount. He may say, "If you love Me, *keep My commandments*," or "Sell all your goods and give them to the poor . . . then follow Me." (But He doesn't necessarily say the *same* thing to everybody.)[9]

Give God an Excuse to Bless You

The bottom line for Naaman's healing wasn't rooted in whether the number God commanded was seven dips or four dips in the Jordan, or to be lightly sprinkled with a purple baby bottle.

It didn't even have anything to do with the inherent virtues of the Jordan River or any other river for that matter. The Jordan River was special not because of its beauty or because of its location. It took on heightened importance only because God chose it as the place for Naaman's miracle.

The issue was obedience. Sometimes God asks us to do things that we do not understand and cannot figure out. Our natural way of handling this is to do everything *but* obey. We would rather make great sacrifices of time, money, or convenience, than simply obey.

Yet God tells us, "To obey is better than sacrifice, in My eyes. Just do what I ask you to do."[10] (In fact, it seems to me that "obey Me" is found more times in Scripture than "obey My commands.")

"Yeah, I know that, Lord, but I prefer to dip six times, not seven." Or, "Okay, Lord, I've taken seven dunks in this muddy river, but now I'm going to dip one more time in this muck just for insurance!"

My personal opinion is that if Naaman had dipped in the river eight times, he would have been stricken with leprosy all over again! It is not a question of doing more; it is a

Obedience is God's excuse to bless you!

question of absolute obedience. Give God an excuse to bless you! Obey absolutely!

Again, if you need to be blessed—if you need some restoration in your life—then give God an excuse to bless you. He is waiting with blessings in His hand. Do you have some obedience to give Him in exchange? Obedience is God's excuse to bless you!

Don't go to God expecting Him to work out a miracle on *your terms.* It is not about you, it is all about Him. We like to control things and put things in neat little predictable boxes. But there is no box big enough to contain, control, or limit God.

We try to attach great significance to what God may consider greatly insignificant, and we downplay what God says is absolutely necessary. It all boils down to one thing: "Are you obedient?"

I Would Rather Keep My Leprosy than Dunk in That Muck

In the beginning, Naaman was probably saying, "I am not going to do it! That is a muddy river. Just look at that stagnant water—it's filthy! I've seen hundreds of rivers that are better than this one! We have two beautiful rivers—Abana and Pharpar—back home in Syria that make this thing look like a sorry mud puddle. I would rather keep my leprosy than dunk in that filthy muck."

Thank God for good staff. One of the Syrian general's lowly servants piped up and said:

> My father, if the prophet had told you to do something great, would you not have done it? How much more then, when he says to you, "Wash, and be clean"?[11]

Imagine the scene—Syria's battle-scarred war hero is dressed in his finest formal attire for what he *thinks* is going to be a grand occasion. He bends down to hear a timid slave say in a shaky voice with trembling knees, "Master Naaman, if that prophet had asked you to do some big thing, would you have done it?"

"Yes, I would have gladly killed one hundred Philistines."

"But how much easier would it be to do this little thing the prophet required?" That lowly servant and the others with him actually humiliated Naaman into obedience!

> **God will gladly sacrifice your comfort to develop your character.**

Do you realize that God—who loves you far more than those slaves loved their Syrian master—will gladly humiliate you into obedience if that is what it takes to help you? He wants the best for you, even when you see no hint of it in your circumstances.

God is less interested in your comfort than He is in your character. God will gladly sacrifice your comfort to develop your character. Why? He is more interested in where you end up than in where you are right now. (Perhaps our proper response should be, "If my humiliation is necessary to bring me to my destination, then so be it.")

Unusual Methods—Who Cares?

Have you noticed that when Jesus ministered to people, He hardly ever prayed for people the same way twice? He didn't want us to build a permanent box labeled "Procedures and Policies for Praying for People."

Jesus prayed for a lot of people so He had to be very inventive to not replicate the *process* but to duplicate the *product*. I suspect that since God created humans, then He is also fully aware of our love for bland repetition, predictability, and reproducible formulas and processes. We seem to value equations and formulas more than relationship.

If we hear that Jesus or even the evangelist in the next town always extended the right index finger and touched sick people on their right temple before miracles occurred, then we're tempted to forget about the faith or obedience involved and start the Holy School of Right Index Finger Miracle Ministry. That is replicating a *process* instead of duplicating the *product*—the restoration or creation of wholeness through God's power.

Jesus seems to have purposely mixed things up to steer us away from simplistic fixations on His techniques. "Okay, I made mud pies yesterday, so today I think I'll stick My finger in some ears and spit on tongues. *The healing line starts right here . . .*"[12]

In fact, just the simple act of mentioning a "healing line" triggers "hot buttons" in some people. If you ask them, they'll say it is undignified to stand up in front of people to receive prayer for their needs. Honestly, I've suffered worse indignities at a hospital just getting medical tests, much less getting healed!

"Can You Spit—a Lot?"

While I know that the Epistles instruct us to use oil when we pray for the sick, interestingly enough, I find no reference where Jesus ever used oil in praying for the sick. But He did use "spit" (or "saliva" for the more politically correct among us).

I don't mean to be gross, but it *is* in the Bible. What if Jesus had spat in the dirt and made mud to anoint every sick and demonized person He prayed for? Most churches would then have a box of dirt from the Holy Land sitting in front of the altar area instead of anointing oil! One of the prerequisites for being an elder would be a positive answer to the question "Can you spit—*a lot*?"

Imagine what might happen when it was time to pray for the sick during a service! The preacher would say, "Elders, join me, please. We're going to pray for people to be healed." At that point, the preacher and all of the elders would begin clearing their throats, preparing the box of holy dirt, and smearing mud on every candidate for prayer!

Jesus did things in different ways so we wouldn't make doctrines out of things He never intended to be doctrines.

Never again would this command be duplicated in the Bible, but here is the result:

> So he went down and dipped seven times in the Jordan, according to the saying of the man of God; and his flesh was restored like the flesh of a little child, and he was clean.[13]

Once Naaman submitted to the indignity of dipping his pristine Syrian robes, water buffalo sandals, and diseased body under the muddy water of the river Jordan, he came out of the water with skin as clear and fresh as a newborn baby's! He also came out with a new attitude about the prophet and Israel's less-than-impressive river.

When God heals you, it is amazing how the very thing that made you mad suddenly makes you glad! Naaman told his astounded military aides and servants, "Turn this chariot around and go straight back to the prophet's house—I'm healed! My skin is restored, it's as soft as a baby's skin."

The Rolls-Royce chariot with the "Syria Rules" license plate slid to a stop in front of Elisha's house and Naaman stepped out. He was dripping wet, he'd ruined the inside of his Rolls-Royce, his sandals were leaking water, his military outfit was messed up, and the feather in his hat was drooping!

Fine Garments from Armani of Syria

He just grinned and announced to the stunned assistant to the prophet, Gehazi:

"I just came to tell the prophet that I'm healed! Tell the preacher to come outside. I've got an offering to give him!

"I want to give him this offering I prepared—I've got a couple of camel-loads of silver, some gold, and some fine garments from Armani of Syria. Can you believe it? I'm healed!"

Gehazi was getting excited. "Hold on a moment, General," he said, and nearly fell over himself scrambling back into the house to find Elisha.

"Master, you know that guy you told to go jump in the river? Well, he did it! I mean, he's back and he is healed! And he's back with an *offering*! He wants to give you an offering—a really *big* offering. If you go out to see him, I'll start carrying in the stuff."

"No, I don't want to see him," Elisha said.

We usually would want to explain away this eccentric action by saying something really spiritual, such as, "Oh, the prophet is on his face before God and cannot come out."

Sleeping Under the Influence (of the Golf Channel)

The problem is that we don't know that. He *could* have been watching the football game or napping under the influence of the golf channel (meaning no offense to avid golfers—it is just what I do).

One day I was in our backyard playing with my little girl. My office called to tell me a high-profile major international minister had phoned. He wanted to talk to me as soon as possible. The problem was that I had set aside that time to be with my daughter, so I told my office:

"I'm really sorry, but tell [and I said the name of the minister] I can't take that call right now. Yes, I know, I know who it is. *I'm in an important meeting right now.*"

When I hung up the phone, my little girl said, "You're not in a meeting, Daddy." And I said, "Yes I am. I am in a meeting with *you*! I set aside this time to spend with you, and I don't care who calls me. They can call me back. I can talk to them anytime, but you are only going to be eleven years old for a little while."

I wish you could have seen her reaction. Later on she told her mother (and who knows how many of her little friends), "My daddy wouldn't talk to them because he was with me!"

We really don't know what Elisha was doing. He may have been playing with his children. In any case, we don't have to make his comment especially "spiritual." All I know is that his answer to the wealthy and powerful Syrian general's offer was:

> "As the LORD lives, before whom I stand, I will receive nothing." And he urged him to take it, but he refused.[14]

"Give Me Some Dirt, Please"

After Naaman dipped seven times in the river, an amazing thing happened. First he offered fabulous gifts of silver and fine garments to the prophet. When the prophet refused any gifts, the Syrian who used to hate the muddy Jordan River actually asked for enough dirt to load up two mules![15] It seems he now loved the mud!

After a destiny-altering encounter, we often value what we used to hate! Evidently he thought he needed "Holy Dirt" from Israel to properly worship God with his offerings.

You Can't Dismiss Church Without an Offering

Elisha may have refused to take anything for the miracle, but Gehazi saw things differently. He just couldn't stand to see that offering walk out the door. *It seems that greed got the best of Gehazi.*

As he watched the Syrian celebrity roll out of the driveway in his custom chariot, something snapped. Syria was one of Israel's hated rivals—and Gehazi thought to himself, *There is no way this Syrian leper should get away with this.*

> But Gehazi, the servant of Elisha the man of God, said, "Look, my master has spared Naaman this Syrian, while not receiving from his hands what he brought; but as the LORD lives, I will run after him and take something from him."[16]

When Elisha the prophet said, "As the LORD lives, *before whom I stand,*" he meant, "God is alive, and I have to give an account to Him for my behavior."

When Gehazi said, "as the LORD lives," he *omitted* the words "before whom I stand" and any other implication of personal relationship and divine accountability. He simply *used the Lord's name as an epitaph*—as a "cussword" for added emphasis!

I Can't Let This Opportunity Go By!

Gehazi's heart must have skipped a beat when he saw the taillights on that Rolls-Royce chariot disappear around the corner. Suddenly he said, "I can't let this opportunity go by!" He sprinted after Naaman's chariot, shouting, "Hey, hey! Hold on, guys; stop! Stop just a minute."

So the Syrian general stopped his caravan of servants and donkeys loaded with gifts. The King James Version of the Bible says with poetic simplicity: "He lighted down from the chariot to meet him, and said, Is all well?"[17] (I can't help but smile when I read that phrase "lighted down.")

Then Gehazi answered, "All is well, *my master hath sent me.*"[18]

Most people would say, "Now, *that* is a lie. His master did not send him!"

I propose Gehazi was telling the absolute truth, only now he was serving a *different* master.

Naaman wanted to give the prophet the big offering he had prepared, so when Gehazi showed up to collect the offering after all and claimed he was sent by the prophet, Naaman *assumed* it was true.

My Master Sent Me . . .

Gehazi then added a second and more elaborate lie to cover his deception. He said, "My Master sent me to tell you about a couple of young Bible school students from Mount Ephraim who need tuition and some new suits. They could use, I would say, about seventy-five pounds of silver as well."[19] (Given the implied high tuition, that must have been *some* school—even by modern standards!)

"What, are you kidding?" Naaman said. "Here, take at *least* 150 pounds of silver; and here are a couple of designer suits for each of those guys." When Naaman saw that Gehazi couldn't carry everything by himself, he told a couple of his servants, "You help Gehazi carry this silver and these garments back to the preacher's house."

Gehazi probably hadn't planned on witnesses, but everything went well until ". . . they got to the tower."

> And *when he came to the tower*, he took them from their hand, and bestowed them in the house: and he let the men go, and they departed.[20]

Towers were always at corners, so Gehazi was afraid that once he and Naaman's slaves rounded the corner, Elisha would see him with the loot. That is when he said, "I'll take it from here."

Gehazi dismissed the Syrian slaves and personally hid the loot once he reached *the tower of presumption*. The Hebrew root word translated as "tower" actually means "to swell, be lifted up, *presume*."[21]

> But he went in, and stood before his master. And Elisha said unto him, Whence comest thou, Gehazi? And he said, Thy servant went no whither.[22]

(I'm still smiling at the archaic but descriptive terms from the King James Version—"whence comest thou" and "no whither.")

Gehazi, Where Have You Been?

Gehazi quickly hid the goods, and thinking his ruse was working, he returned to stand before Elisha. Then the old prophet turned those piercing eyes on him as he said, "Gehazi, where have you been?"

"Oh, nowhere." (This is my own translation of "no whither.")

The trap of God was about to snap shut and Gehazi was about to learn a lesson about the all-knowing, all-seeing God that he would never forget.

> Then he [Elisha] said to him, "Did not my heart go with you when the man turned back from his chariot to meet you? Is it time to receive money and to receive clothing, olive groves and vineyards, sheep and oxen, male and female servants?"[23]

The prophet was saying, "Gehazi, don't even start. I know where you've been, I know what you've done, and I know what you hid away in secret. Gehazi, this is not the time for you to be taking the offering."

I mean, the old prophet went off on him! He started talking about things Gehazi didn't even receive. Vineyards, olive groves, sheep, and oxen!

Have you ever thought a preacher was overreacting?

Perhaps Elisha was illuminating the next levels that Gehazi's behavior would escalate to if it was left unchecked. Sometimes God has to put a painful halt in our lives before more damage is done. Gehazi is about to "hit bottom." This is the "fall" we were talking about.

Elisha made one of the most shocking pronouncements of judgment in the Old Testament:

> "Therefore the leprosy of Naaman shall cling to you and your descendants forever." And he [Gehazi] went out from his presence leprous, as white as snow.[24]

Gehazi received one of the speediest trials in human history and his sentence was carried out instantly! The Bible says Gehazi walked out of the prophet's house a leper, "as white as snow."

In Gehazi's lifetime, no phrase was more feared than "You've got leprosy." This man didn't simply contract leprosy, where it begins with a suspicious little patch of unusual skin. I believe Gehazi was instantly *covered* with leprosy at the same level that Naaman had when it washed away in the river Jordan.

When he received "the leprosy of Naaman," Gehazi immediately received it at the same *advanced stage* marked by the same *bleached skin* that Naaman had just before he stepped into the Jordan's muddy waters. It was literally *"the"* leprosy of Naaman.

Accosted by His Own Mistake

In one life-crushing instant, Gehazi was accosted by his own mistake. Suddenly, Gehazi's secret triumph was replaced by public tragedy. Fear replaced faith, and despair displaced hope. *One error in judgment, one bad decision, and life as he knew it was over.*

Do you remember that sentence? It is from the beginning of this "oops" chapter. I'm sure that Gehazi wished he had never said what he said, or did what he did. But you can't undo mistakes.

This high-ranking servant to the greatest prophet of the day literally turned as white as snow, totally encrusted with the flaky skin cells and oozing sores indicative of advanced-stage leprosy.

> Obedience is God's excuse to bless you, and disobedience can be God's permission to curse you.

It all happened because Gehazi illicitly took silver and garments that were not his. Gehazi illegally and presumptuously intercepted riches and valuable goods God intended to be *returned* to their source. He literally contaminated himself with illicit goods, presumptuous disobedience, and the attempt to deceive God's anointed prophet.

If obedience is God's excuse to bless you, then is disobedience

God's permission to curse you? Gehazi's actions placed him under the curse of leprosy.

The prophet asked him just before pronouncing Gehazi's doom, "Is it a *time* to receive money, and to receive garments?"[25] The problem was not the money or the garments; it was the "time."

He was banned from society, condemned to suffer gradually increasing disfigurement and perpetual pain followed by certain and premature death. His future was over, just because he misjudged the time.

An Entire Family Line Extinguished in One Sentence

What more could be done to punish this man? Closely examine the prophet's final words to Gehazi. Something much worse *did* happen: "The leprosy therefore of Naaman shall cleave unto thee, and unto *thy seed for ever*."[26]

Have you ever pondered the reality of the word "forever"? Perhaps you've experienced the depression of "forever" in your life. Consider Gehazi's "forever" curse. His *seed*, his entire family line of male descendants, was virtually extinguished in one brief sentence!

When Gehazi went home, I suspect he discovered his things were already thrown out into the dusty street, along with his sons and their belongings. Each son was instantly infected with the same disease—and with the same severity—as his father.

It is always dangerous to second-guess God. Presumption is the leprosy of the soul. Never try to live your life and pretend to be a child of God *while leaning on another person's intimacy* with Divinity.

Gehazi lived in the same house with a prophet, and he *thought* he understood it all. So much so that he made a fatal judgment call. There were other times when Elisha gladly accepted gifts from people, but this time he made it clear he would not take any silver or garments, and he implied it was by divine direction. *Without a reason why!* Sometimes the mark of maturity is to obey without a reason why.

When Gehazi presumed to second-guess the prophet of God, he opened the door for sin. This whole mess began when Satan persuaded Eve to second-guess God, and that act (with Adam's willing participation) opened the door for the fatal virus of disobedience to infect the entire human race.

Normally, when you read in God's Word that a prophet pronounced such a fatal and "forever" permanent penalty,

Presumption is the leprosy of the soul.

wouldn't you suspect that Gehazi's days were over? He seems to quietly disappear from the biblical narrative and fade into anonymity at that point.

While virtually every Sunday school scholar knows about Naaman dipping in the Jordan seven times, you are about to discover that his story really serves as a background for a miraculous incident far greater than Naaman's cure!

As great as the turnaround story of the Syrian leader was, he was really just a bit-part player for what may be *"the ultimate comeback"* of the Old Testament—a miracle that may forever transform your understanding of restoration.

CHAPTER 5

This Could Be a Miserable Year
Just Forward My Mail to "Hell"

Naaman the Syrian and his royal caravan were barely out of sight. The former leper's loud, uninhibited shouts of joy could still be heard echoing in the distance when Elisha's servant, Gehazi, saw his life shatter before his eyes.

It happened in the time it took to say one short sentence: "The *leprosy* of Naaman shall cling to you and your descendants *forever.*"[1]

He didn't see it coming. Gehazi was in complete shock as he stumbled out of the cool inner chamber of the prophet's house. He shivered at the memory of Elisha's smoldering eyes in those final moments.

What do you say after you say "oops"? Typically, the next exclamatory phrase is, "Uh-oh." Suddenly, it all begins to sink in that you have just entered a miserable phase of your life. Have you ever felt like saying, "Just forward my mail to 'hell,' because that's where I'm going to be living"?

I'm not just speaking of a time when you are in the proverbial "doghouse" because of a spat with your spouse, or when your boss was temporarily angry with you. No, this is the *ultimate stroke of doom*, the final blow to any hope for normality in the immediate future. "She's not just mad . . . she *left.*" Your boss is not just upset—"you're *fired!*" Now your future is clouded with misery.

How did Gehazi become so blinded to the stark supernatural power of God? Somehow he became too familiar with what others considered holy and often did not understand.

The human desire to hide, shift, and justify is strong. Gehazi must have struggled with his "mistake" and the seriousness of the penalty.

> The idea to receive the gifts from the Syrian seemed so easy, and everything happened so smoothly.
>
> The old prophet said he didn't want the stuff; and the foreign leper was so happy over his miracle that he really didn't care about it either. Naaman had plenty of money. After all, it was just another 150-plus pounds to caravan all the way back to Syria over rugged mountain passes. What was the harm? Hadn't he done the man a favor?

One name should have exploded in his memory: *Achan*. Every Jew could recite by heart the story about the man who took for himself what had been set aside for God. Immediately after the Israelites watched the massive walls of Jericho come down, Achan secretly looted illicit silver and gold from the rubble. That action had been banned by God.

His secret sin of touching what God had openly declared off-limits brought a curse on the entire nation. Every Hebrew child was carefully taught to fear the judgment unleashed on those who committed "the sin of Achan."[2]

How Did the Old Prophet See Me?

What did that ancient name of greed and shame have to do with anything? Gehazi had just committed *the sin of Achan* . . . the prophet made it clear there was something "off-limits" about this silver and those garments.

How many times in the ensuing miserable years did Gehazi rehearse his story to himself in order to justify his actions?

I'm no Achan—didn't I wash the hands of the man of God? I didn't steal anything from anybody—I just helped myself to free stuff. And I probably would have used it for some good.

Sure, I didn't count on the two Syrian slaves helping me with the stuff; but once we got close to the corner I just sent them back to Naaman.

It was a simple thing to quickly move the goods into the house. All I had to do was hide them—uh, store them—in the cool chamber cut into the wall just behind the large water pots. **But how did the old prophet see me?**

Unconsciously scratching the spreading itchy spots on his face and neck, Gehazi shuffled hurriedly toward his house while avoiding anyone he saw. Every word and nuance of his encounter with the prophet was burned into his memory.

Gehazi forgot that covetousness is as bad as idolatry. It's not what you did, but how did God see it?

"Where have you been, Gehazi?"

"Your servant went nowhere."

"Did not my heart go with you, when the man turned from his chariot to meet you? Is it a time to receive money and to receive clothes and olive groves and vineyards and sheep and oxen and male and female servants?

"Therefore, the leprosy of Naaman shall cleave to you and to your descendants forever . . . forever . . . forever."[3]

Stunned by His Sudden Fall

No one really knows how Gehazi felt, but it stunned him to experience the *suddenness of his fall*, the *permanence* of his sentence, and the *extension of leprosy's sorrow* to his sons and his grandsons.

It was as if he was told, "By the way, Gehazi, don't worry about not being around to enjoy your children's future. They've already got leprosy too." It wasn't fair!

Life is not always fair. "Why not just punish *me*?" The pain of watching others suffer for mistakes *you* made is often unbearable.

Gehazi's arrest, trial, and conviction were swift enough to make his head spin. But the *instantaneous* sentence of leprosy stunned him. He went from high to lower than low in less than one minute!

It takes time to develop leprosy, but just as God can accelerate mercy, He can accelerate judgment. Perhaps when you were younger, you experienced the "acceleration of judgment" on a smaller scale when your parents made the statement "That's it. I've had it!" (When they make the statement "*I've* had it," that usually means *you've* had it.)

Someone other than Gehazi also learned firsthand just how *quickly* failure follows false victory. Another prophet once said of that one's swift fall, "I saw Satan *fall* like lightning from heaven."[4]

Elsewhere, it is written:

> "How you are fallen from heaven, O Lucifer, son of the morning! How you are cut down to the ground, you who weakened the nations! For you have said in your heart: '*I will* ascend into heaven, *I will* exalt my throne above the stars of God; *I will* also sit on the mount of the congregation on the farthest sides of the north; *I will* ascend above the heights of the clouds, *I will* be like the Most High.' Yet *you shall* be brought down to Sheol, to the lowest depths of the Pit . . ."
>
> The LORD of hosts has sworn, saying, "Surely, as I have thought, so it shall come to pass, and as I have purposed, so it *shall stand*."[5]

This is what happens when the "*I will's*" meet the "*shall stand's*"! God accelerated Lucifer's judgment.

Naaman's Leprosy Latched onto Gehazi

I don't believe Gehazi went through the normal process and progressive stages of leprosy. The Scriptures imply Gehazi picked up the full-blown leprosy right where Naaman dropped it off! Accelerated judgment!

The prophet said, "The leprosy of Naaman shall cleave to you *and to your descendants forever . . .*" It doesn't get much worse than this.

If it is said someone experienced "the ultimate comeback or turnaround," then it is also understood that somehow that same person has experienced the pain and sorrow of coming to *the ultimate dead end.* You cannot experience an ultimate turnaround without realizing you have to come to the ultimate dead end.

At this moment, we see no hint of any comeback or turnaround. Gehazi has experienced the worst scenario possible—a fate most would consider worse than death, for it was a living and lingering death of sorts. He was cursed "by the word of the Lord." The prophet said he and his sons would have leprosy forever.

Perhaps you've had a professional counselor tell you, "I don't know how you are going to repair this relationship. Your situation may be irretrievable."

It is one thing to hear a degreed counselor pronounce a dark future over your life. But what if the curse was leveled over your life by a renowned prophet of God?

Elisha received the double mantle of the prophet Elijah's office. He prophesied the birth of a son to a barren Shunammite woman, and later restored that teenage son to life after he died prematurely. He orchestrated the defeat of a Moabite army and the surrender of the Syrian army, and then God used him to perform the miraculous healing of Naaman, Syria's commanding general of the army.[6]

This man was the acknowledged *voice of God* to Gehazi's generation. When Elisha cursed you, it was universally understood that *God Himself* had cursed you.

Move forward nearly three thousand years. What if someone with the stature of Billy Graham or Mother Teresa publicly pronounced doom over you and your family *forever*? Elisha the prophet essentially told Gehazi publicly, "You will have to live with the consequences of this bad decision *forever!*"

If you feel permanently cursed at this moment, then perhaps you can identify with Gehazi. Perhaps it was not a minister; maybe it was your boss or your spouse.

Just how cursed was Gehazi? Moses and the Levitical law were clear:

> As for the leper who has the infection, his clothes shall be torn, and the hair of his head shall be uncovered, and he shall cover his mustache and cry, "Unclean! Unclean!"
>
> He shall remain unclean all the days during which he has the infection; he is unclean. He shall live alone; his dwelling shall be outside the camp.[7]

Do you hear and see the words in these passages on leprosy? "Infection ... torn ... uncovered ... unclean ... shall live alone ... outside the camp."

Miriam's Flesh Was "Half Eaten Away" by Leprosy

The curse of leprosy was so devastating that it would cause Moses to have a desperate reaction when his sister was struck with leprosy for her rebellion. He wasn't talking about someone who was merely "ritually" unclean, he was crying out in desperation to God for divine intervention in a medical as well as a spiritual crisis:[8]

> "Oh, do not let her be *like one dead, whose flesh is half eaten away* when he comes from his mother's womb!"
>
> Moses cried out to the LORD, saying, "O God, heal her, I pray!"[9]

Moses was one of the Bible's most detailed writers and most accurate prophets. It was to Moses God delivered the Ten Commandments, the "Mosaic Law," and the Levitical ordinances in minute detail. This righteous man simply told God what he saw.

Miriam, Moses's sister, wasn't merely struck with a flaky skin condition that would go away in a day or two! No, this woman was being eaten alive by a wasting, consuming disease that went much further than merely afflicting the woman's skin with itching and flaky spots. She didn't just have "ashy" skin that could be cured by a liberal application of olive oil.

Leprosy: Death on the Layaway Plan

Some say a decree of leprosy was a sentence just short of a death sentence. You could say it was a "death sentence on layaway." Others would say death was easier than leprosy.

In any case, to say leprosy was a dreaded disease is an understatement. You didn't live with leprosy, you died with it. Gehazi must have asked himself, "Why did it have to be leprosy?"

No other disease in Old Testament society brought such destruction and desolation. Thousands of years before people detected or suspected the existence of germs, God warned Moses about a mysterious super disease unlike anything the world had ever known.

Leprosy came to be recognized as one of the most feared judgments of God, one that was reserved for people guilty of presumption and open trespass against His authority and commands.

As I said, if modern-day cancer were as *contagious* as the typical cold virus, then everyone who lay dying on a hospital bed from cancer would suffer alone.

Now, again imagine the extremely contagious nature of the common cold, the stigma of the virtually 100 percent fatal AIDS/HIV virus, and the paralyzing fear produced by a cancer diagnosis—**all rolled up into one!** You are just beginning to understand the impact of the disease transferred from Naaman to Gehazi and his male heirs.

Leprosy in certain stages was fatal, fearful, painful, progressive, humanly incurable, disfiguring, isolating, and extremely contagious.

This biblical disease started to kill its victims from the moment it first appeared. The first symptoms to appear were often dry scaly patches of skin on the forehead or the back of the head and neck. Then it began to methodically eat *inward*, moving from skin to muscle and sinew, to the bones and inner body organs.

Lepers Lacked the Feeling to Protect Their Feet and Extremities

Leprosy was especially effective at destroying nerve cells, depriving its victims of the all-important warning sign of *pain*. The victims couldn't feel what was going on in their extremities, but they *did* feel phantom pain where their toes, fingers, and facial features *used to be*.

What the disease didn't destroy, the destruction of the nerves destroyed through an endless series of accidents damaging the unfeeling tissues on the feet and hands, which could lead to gangrene and massive infection.

Leprosy is one of the most disfiguring diseases ever to afflict the human race. It may eat away the victim's fingers and toes, nose or ears; moving digit by digit, one facial feature after another.

Many believe the ancient form of leprosy was very similar to modern leprosy, now called Hansen's disease.[10]

Naaman's Leprosy Fell with Fresh Fury on Gehazi

The leprosy that nearly destroyed Naaman's life fell with fresh fury on Gehazi the servant of the prophet of God. Not since the sin and execution of Achan had anyone been struck so hard for touching forbidden silver and garments.

When the full-blown leprosy of Naaman came upon Gehazi as Elisha prophesied, the man who washed the prophet's hands was instantly doomed to the life of a leper and banned from polite society.[11]

Identity theft existed long before the arrival of computer hackers, "viruses," and spyware . . . it was called *leprosy*. When this silent killer leaped from Naaman's body to capture Elisha's servant, the man's name was instantly stolen from him. His entire identity changed in seconds from Gehazi—which means "valley of vision"—to simply leper (which means "smite" or "scourge" in the Hebrew).[12]

His vocation immediately changed from "servant to the prophet" to the "homeless beggar with leprosy." His clothing changed by law, and so did his address.

For several years, Gehazi had enjoyed the unique privilege of sharing the address of Israel's most powerful and feared leader. Elisha was even more powerful and influential than the king of Israel! (That is why we find the elders of the nation conferring with Elisha instead of the king.)[13]

It would be the same as your address being the White House or Buckingham Palace instead of the address of your humble family residence. All of that changed in one day.

His Forwarding Address Became Hell

The moment Gehazi appeared in daylight with full-blown leprosy, it was as if his forwarding address became "hell."[14] Lepers always lived *outside* the city, away from the village, separated from any camp occupied by "normal" people. They were "dead men walking," and no one was interested in joining their club.

Every Jew knew the stories, tall tales, and urban legends about "Gehenna," Jerusalem's town dump, where the trash fires never went out, day or night. Gehazi didn't live in Jerusalem, but he lived in another Jewish capital city called Samaria. It, no doubt, had one of those places too. That is, a trash dump, the type of place where lepers lived.

One thing is absolutely for certain—Gehazi was banned from cohabiting with the living because he became one of the living dead. His forwarding address changed from the prophet's house to outside the city walls. Living off the refuse of the citizens.

It was every city's dumping ground, the no-man's-land under the freeway overpasses, in the sewer systems, and near the railroad yards—inhabited by the desperate, discarded, disreputable, disgusting refuse of society and "polite company." Once you land in the dump called Gehenna, your name is wiped from memory.

By Jesus's day, Gehenna was so foul and desecrated that He and His disciples used it as their number one earthly picture and prophetic model for *hell*, that literal place of unquenchable fire, darkness, and divine judgment.

Welcome to Gehazi's hell, the neighborhood where dying is actually easier than living. Leprosy was nothing less than a living death spent in total separation from family, friends, support, or community acceptance. Your future contains nothing but an existence marked by loneliness, pain, and hopelessness.

You were totally isolated from society in Gehazi's hellish Gehenna because you could not live inside a walled city ever again. At best, you were doomed to live in the country or to live with other lepers in "hell" just *outside* any city limit. Living just outside human interaction is hell. You can see the community; you just can't participate in it.

If you had leprosy and you loved your children, you would never hug them again. *Is that a picture of your life?* The literal proof of your love was to demonstrate how far you would stay away from them rather than how close you could get to them.

Identify Yourself: Unclean, Unclean!

When anyone came close, the Law demanded that you identify your condition in a loud voice while hiding your face and beard: "Unclean, unclean! Don't get close."

The residents of a leper's Gehenna literally lived on the scrap heaps and sanitation dumps of society. The more compassionate (and daring) members of the society of the clean *might* leave food scraps for you from a safe distance.

Most of the time, I suspect, the residents of Gehazi's "neighborhood" lived on the rancid leftovers and unsanitary rubbish thrown over the walls or just outside the gates of the city of Samaria.

Not only do you die, but you die alone. And you die a disfiguring and painful death. Loneliness itself is a disfiguring condition. It lines the face with sorrow and causes eyes once bright with joy to sink deep into the eye sockets, sentinels of sorrow upon sorrow harbored by the lonely and embittered soul within.

Do you feel alone, disfigured, and dishonored in your pain? Are life and joy draining from your soul and personality?

The lepers who lost their extremities could no longer balance themselves because they didn't have any toes to apply counterbalancing pressure (and they couldn't *feel* any surface with their feet anyway). They would find it difficult or impossible to grasp or hold small objects, which made it nearly impossible to care for themselves adequately. It was an ugly existence.

With each passing day, the disabling effects of neuropathy (death of the nerves) continue to aggressively advance from the extremities of the toes and fingers toward the heart.

The curse of numbness robs its victims of freedom, independence, and the ability to interact with the world around them. We even see this curse attacking the souls of our Prozac society, inducing a paralyzing, crippling numbness of spirit—producing an unfeeling, uncaring, numb nation.

That is what leprosy did. It isolated, disfigured, and destroyed. I don't want to cheaply provoke a tear in your eye, but as you read this, is something crying out in your heart? *That's me! I feel stripped bare, isolated, alone, and victimized by the ultimate identity theft. I am not what I used to be! I made mistakes, so what do I do now?*

What Do You Do When Your Mail Is Forwarded to Hell?

Gehazi surrendered to the numbing nightmare of living in hell on earth. His last good memories of Elisha's ministry included seeing a sopping wet Naaman rejoicing over his baby-soft skin and the miracle of seeing a dead boy raised and restored to his amazed mother. As year ran into year of cumulative misery, perhaps those memories were growing dimmer by the month.

Have you ever felt such pain in your life that you felt as if your present address was hell? Have you wondered whether dying would actually be easier than living? (It isn't!)

There is One who can show you the way out.

It reminds me of a scene in a movie about the life of Mahatma Gandhi, the late East Indian leader. One scene in particular captures the power of what you are about to discover through Gehazi's life.

A political bloodbath drives Gandhi to conduct a public hunger strike to the death unless the Muslims and the Hindus make peace between themselves.

Although Gandhi was a Hindu, he conducted the hunger strike in the home of a Muslim in Calcutta. He is so weak and emaciated that his friends fear he is dying. The Muslim governor of Bengal, who helped incite the bloody religious riots in Calcutta, is so repentant (and afraid of losing such a famous and powerful leader on his watch) that he is willing to do all he can to help.

Then a group of would-be rioting Hindu murderers walk in and surrender their weapons. The wildest looking of them all bursts in and almost throws bread on Gandhi. "Here! Eat!" he shouts. "I am going to hell; but I do not wish to have your death on my soul!"

Gandhi feebly whispers to him, "Only God decides who goes to hell. Tell me, why do you say you are going to hell?"

"I killed a [Muslim] small child! I dashed his head against the wall because they killed my little one."

Gandhi says, "*I will tell you a way out of hell*: You find a Muslim child whose parents have been killed. Then you and your wife bring him up as your own."

With a look of disbelief on his face, the Hindu man solemnly bends low to touch Gandhi's feet with his forehead before leaving without another word.[15]

One *greater* than Gandhi said:

"I know a way out of hell."

This leader, teacher, philosopher, and Savior didn't simply lead us on a tortuous path of "self-enlightenment." He broke open a door where there was no door by laying down His life at death's dead end!

This King of kings took upon Himself the leprosy of our sins, and He was rejected and denied burial residence in any royal cemetery. Many thought He was finished and gone for good, and His battered body was placed outside the city in a borrowed tomb.

But *He had plans after the weekend.* He rose again and destroyed the power of sin—*and* leprosy—forever.

One could think that once such a nightmare sentence was pronounced over Gehazi that he would be finished too. However, I noticed something as I was reading through the rest of the Book of Second Kings that turns the tables on everything we *thought* we knew about Gehazi the leper. It is time for "the rest of the story . . ."

In the meantime, understand that it doesn't matter what valley or garbage dump you're living in, or how miserable this year may be. Jesus is saying, "I know *a way out of hell—follow Me!*"

CHAPTER 6

The Ultimate Comeback!
"He's Back!"

Gehazi, the servant of Elisha, had already fallen into the oblivion of failure. My personal thought process consigned him to the blacklist of failure in biblical history.

As I continued to read the biblical history of Israel's prophets and kings, Elisha's servant became just another mortal marker of failure. He was a human monument to the power of greed over the human soul and its inevitable downfall.

After all, this man was caught with both of his hands in the proverbial cookie jar of ill-gotten gain. He wasn't just an embezzler. He stole ministry money! That makes Gehazi virtually unrestorable. He was judged and found wanting, with the prophet of God pronouncing the consequences of his sin immediately. This man definitely had a "speedy trial."

However, the implementation of his sentence was anything but swift. Gehazi's journey to death as a leper would be private, painful, isolated, and hopeless. It seemed appropriate in my mind that the former servant of Elisha *fade* from the scene, as the narrative of God's kingdom advanced.

That is exactly the problem—it seems so logical and deserved that I almost didn't notice something that turned the tables on everything

I *thought* I knew about Gehazi. I stumbled across this clue about the leper as I read through the Book of Second Kings.

It may not be appropriate to quote Yogi Berra beside the Bible, but it fits: "It ain't over till it's over."

There are two people whose dramatic declarations have come to define "comeback" in the culture of two generations.

General Douglas MacArthur stood on the shore of the Philippines in the early stages of World War II, with overwhelming Japanese forces bearing down upon his outnumbered and outgunned troops struggling to complete an emergency retreat. Just before he stepped away from that Philippine beach to board a ship, he announced, "I shall return." (He made good on his promise and recaptured the Philippine Islands later in the war.)

To our more contemporary culture, Arnold Schwarzenegger made movie history when his character growled in a heavy Austrian accent the phrase, "I'll be back!"

Have you ever made that type of statement? (Maybe only to yourself.) "I shall return" or "I'll be back"? Perhaps Gehazi mumbled it to himself a million times, or said it to others thousands of times. Perhaps nobody believed him.

Here's the rest of the story . . .

In the verses after the judgment descended on Gehazi in Second Kings chapter 5, I continued to read about the prophets and kings who led Israel. Chapter 6, chapter 7, chapter 8 . . . I had nearly fallen asleep, when something jarred me out of my "auto mode" and sent an alarm to my brain, warning me that I had passed something worth noticing.

It was time to shift out of neutral and really examine something I had just read. It only took a moment to find what had triggered the mental alarm.

There it was, a *single word* slipped into a passage in the eighth chapter of the Book of Second Kings. It seemed to be completely out of sequence for some reason. I read it again, blinked, and then read it a third time just to make sure I was accurately reading the passage.

I'd already slipped past it and was well into the story of the wealthy but childless woman who prepared a place for Elisha the prophet and was rewarded with a son.

When the boy suddenly died while in the fields with his father, the woman took her dead son to the prophet's quarters she'd built and called for Elisha.

Elisha raised the boy from the dead in one of the greatest of the Old Testament miracles and then warned the woman to take her son out of the country for seven years—he predicted a great famine was coming to the land.

The mother and her son immediately obeyed, but when she returned seven years later, she discovered squatters occupying her lands and home!

It was when this woman and her son entered the king's court to petition for legal help evicting the squatters that this *single word* riveted my attention.

> It came to pass, at the end of seven years, that the woman returned from the land of the Philistines; and she went to make an appeal to the king for her house and for her land.
>
> Then the king talked with Gehazi, the servant of the man of God, saying, "Tell me, please, all the great things Elisha has done."[1]

He's Back!

Wait a minute! Who? Where did this man come from? As improbable as it seems—*Gehazi is back!* If you came across this passage while casually skimming through your Bible, you probably wouldn't suspect anything unusual. *Unless*, that is, you remembered that this "Gehazi" character was banished to the hell of incurable leprosy *three* chapters earlier!

So what is Gehazi the leper doing here? What happened between then and now to produce this incredible turnaround? Is it a mistake?

Is this really the same miserable man? Is this evidence of the ultimate comeback, or just a fluke?

There is no doubt about it: *this is the same Gehazi.* He is identified by the phrase "*the servant of Elisha.*" This phrase is in the "present tense" in the original language of this Scripture passage, not the "had been" mode. That means he was apparently *restored* to his original position with Elisha along with an apparent promotion to the throne room of the king! What grace!

We can see he is back, but how did he get there? This story has some missing chapters! How did Gehazi make the ultimate comeback?

All available previous evidence pointed to this man spending the rest of his life in leprosy's clutches. Who or what commuted the prophet's death sentence decree that Gehazi die a leper? How did he regain the *present-tense title* "servant to Elisha" and then step into a royal position at the king's side? Was he now the king's official court liaison to the prophet?

The first rule of Bible interpretation is to establish the *context* of what is being said or happening. The last time we heard from this man, his greatest worry for the future was likely to be finding ways to keep his fingers from falling off.[2]

By Levitical law and prophetic decree, Gehazi had to stay away— far away—from everyone except other lepers for the *rest of his life*! In my mind, the events surrounding the healing of Naaman the Syrian and the cursing of Gehazi were signed, sealed, and "forever."

God Loves a Great Mystery

So why do we read about Gehazi conversing in close proximity with a king three chapters after leprosy covered his body?

Perhaps God loves a great mystery. I read somewhere that He even called the gospel of Jesus Christ—His grand plan to restore humanity—a "great *mystery*."[3]

Part of the art of crafting a good mystery is the skillful presentation and management of time and events. How do you tell part of a story while carefully withholding and concealing the dramatic climax for the very end?

We see it in countless celebrated classics, modern novels, short stories, and award-winning motion pictures. They begin a story at or very near *the end*—usually when things look their worst. Then they jump backward in time to tell the story forward to its final dramatic conclusion. Only then do all of the pieces come together for maximum impact.

The Author of our existence used this technique long before human civilization existed. He said, "I am God, and there is none like Me, *declaring the end from the beginning*, and from ancient times *things that are not yet done*."[4]

Why should we be surprised to find a "surprise ending" in the Bible? The Book of Life is filled with them. Nevertheless, I was surprised to come across Gehazi doing unexpected things in an unusual place with an unlikely cast of characters.

Gehazi's name appears in the Bible a total of twelve times. Three times Gehazi's name shows up during his fateful interaction with Naaman, the Syrian leper, and his theft of silver and garments.

We have already considered Gehazi's sin and fall. After that encounter, Gehazi began to die a day at a time under the scourge of leprosy, while struggling to survive in the dark shadows and continual weight of his failure and the curse of God on his life.

His Life Was Linked to an Unlikely Pair

My search for answers led me to research all nine of the other instances where Gehazi appears in the Scriptures. What I confirmed in each instance is that Gehazi's life is somehow linked to a very unlikely pair of people—a Shunammite woman and her son.

When the king of Israel asked Gehazi to tell him of all the great things Elisha had done, this mother and son showed up in Gehazi's reply because they were part of Elisha's greatest miracle:

> And Gehazi was telling the king about the time Elisha had brought a boy back to life . . .[5]

Good information was hard to come by in those days when news traveled only as fast as the swiftest horse, and when its accuracy decreased exponentially with each added person in the information chain. (The accuracy problem *still* plagues us today!)

You get the feeling this king was excited to finally discover an eyewitness to a genuine miracle who was literally right under his royal nose!

No Clue as to How or Where He Came From

We are sure this is Gehazi doing the talking, but we don't have a clue how or where the king connected to this former leper, who was now his throne room confidant.

Gehazi tells the story of Elisha's greatest miracle by starting at the beginning. Elisha was a traveling prophet, an itinerant preacher and holy man. So he was blessed by the open hospitality of a wealthy Shunammite woman and her husband. He regularly spent the night in the prophet's chamber they had attached to their house exclusively for his use.

That is when he asked his personal assistant, Gehazi, to consult with the woman about any needs she might have. She was so well connected financially and politically, that she didn't need any material or political favors. It was Gehazi who drew on his shrewd powers of observation and suggested that perhaps she might like a son. She had been unable to bear children and she was married to a much older man.

The prophet acted on Gehazi's suggestion and prophesied that the childless Shunammite woman would have a son at about the same time the following year. The woman's response was essentially, "Don't tease me."

The son was born exactly as promised, but as he neared his teen years, he suddenly collapsed with severe head pain while visiting his father and the farmhands in the harvest fields. The workers took him to his mother, and the boy died in her arms.

The mother carried her son's body into the prophet's chambers beside her house and laid him on the prophet's bed. (There is some truth to the old adage "You've made your bed, now lie in it.") This woman had staked her life and future on pursuing the blessing of God through the prophet. Now she piled her sorrow onto the bed she'd made before God and for her prophet. Then she rushed out to find old Elisha. It is at this point that Gehazi entered the picture once again.

Elisha was on a mountaintop when he saw the woman approaching from a distance. He told Gehazi to run and meet her, and to ask if all was well with her family.

She told Gehazi everything was fine, but when she finally reached the prophet she dropped to her knees and caught hold of his feet in desperation.

He Began to Shove the Woman Away

Gehazi moved forward quickly and began to shove the woman away from Elisha (he was probably angry, embarrassed, and possibly jealous that she had told him everything was fine when she now made it clear to the prophet that she was obviously upset). Elisha quickly told Gehazi to leave her be.

The religious barrier builders without a clue about spiritual relationship, often try to shove people away and limit access to the presence of God—even though they know so little about the subject. The disciples tried to remove children who wanted to sit on Jesus's knee; they made sure non-Jewish outsiders had to *ask* before being allowed to see Jesus.[6]

When Elisha found out the Shunammite woman's son had died, he threw his staff to Gehazi and told him to run ahead to the woman's house and lay the staff on the dead boy's body.[7]

In short, nothing that Gehazi did worked. The prophet's staff was powerless in the faithless servant's hands. Gehazi *had* to be frustrated.

Once Elisha arrived and heard Gehazi's report of failure, he locked himself in the room with the dead boy. He prayed for the boy twice—the first time the boy's body warmed up, and the second time he sneezed seven times and was restored to full health.

She Ignored Gehazi's Request

Once again Elijah called for Gehazi, and had him call in the mother. When she saw that her son had been raised from the dead, she apparently ignored Gehazi's request that she take the boy and go her way.

The Shunammite woman went directly to the man of God to *thank him for praying for her son.* Only then did she take her boy in her arms.[8]

It seems Elisha wasn't done. Once he had healed and raised the boy from the dead through the power of God, *Elisha added something a little extra.*

In Louisiana, where I am from, we have a French phrase for that "added extra," it's called "lagniappe" (lán-yap). When you go to the store to buy something in the Cajun country of southern Louisiana, they often give you an extra—you just received a little *lagniappe.* If you purchase a dozen eggs, then for a little *lagniappe* the grocers or store-keepers will give you one extra egg.

(This old French custom from the days of the Louisiana Purchase is very similar to the English custom of a "baker's dozen" where a baker may throw in thirteen donuts or rolls instead of just twelve.)

After Elisha raised the boy from the dead, for a little lagniappe, he told the boy's mother, "By the way, you need to take your family and move out of town for a while. A terrible famine is coming to Israel. You can come back safely in seven years."

> *It's not enough to receive a miracle. Preserve what you receive!*

Why would Elisha add this additional advice? What would you do if God used you to raise that boy from the dead and you knew he would probably face death again through starvation?

Sometimes it takes unprecedented effort to preserve what God has given you. That truth often just doesn't register with some people who get blessed or have something restored to them by God. You can almost hear God say, "Look, I restored it to you! Now the least you could do is take all possible precautions to preserve what I've given you."

Let me ask you this: If God raised your son or daughter from the dead and then said, "You need to leave here for seven years," would you take the risk to come back in six years and nine months? (I wouldn't either!) I believe the Shunammite woman and her son returned to Israel exactly seven years later.

Unfortunately, upon their return she and her family discovered that squatters had taken over their property. Squatters are people who illegally start occupying property that doesn't belong to them without the permission of its legal owners. These squatters obviously didn't want to leave. They were in her house, eating from her fields, and now she would have to have them evicted.

The Prophet Made a Promise—It was Time for an Eviction

The king held all legal authority in his hand, so the Bible tells us that the Shunammite woman and her son sought an audience with the king over their squatter problem. The prophet had made a promise and they wanted their land back.

> Elisha had told the woman whose son he had brought back to life, "Take your family and move to some other place, for the LORD has called for a famine on Israel that will last for seven years."
>
> So the woman did as the man of God instructed. She took her family and lived in the land of the Philistines for seven years.
>
> After the famine ended she returned to the land of Israel, and she went to see the king about getting back her house and land.
>
> *As she came in, the king was talking with Gehazi, the servant of the man of God.* The king had just said, "Tell me some stories about the great things Elisha has done."
>
> And Gehazi was telling the king about the time Elisha had brought a boy back to life. *At that very*

moment, the mother of the boy walked in to make her appeal to the king. "Look, my lord!" Gehazi exclaimed. "Here is the woman now, and this is her son—the very one Elisha brought back to life!"

"Is this true?" the king asked her. And she told him that it was. So he directed one of his officials to see to it that everything she had lost was restored to her, including the value of any crops that had been harvested during her absence.[9]

More Interested in the Reappearance than in the Coincidence

Most of the people who read these passages quickly notice the amazing "coincidence" that this woman and her son would walk into the throne room at the *exact moment* Gehazi was telling their story to the king. It is amazing timing, but it was no coincidence. Yet, that is not what caught my attention.

It was the sudden appearance of the "Mysterious Missing Man from Hell" that baffled me. How did Gehazi show up again in the biblical narrative? I thought he had been relegated to a leprous excommunication! In fact, it's possible that by now, seven years later, Gehazi could have been dead!

But here he is! Did I miss a part of the story somehow? Are there pages missing from my Bible?

The last time we heard about Gehazi, he was tangled up in the nets of pride and greed while illicitly receiving silver and garments from a grateful Naaman the Syrian, who was healed of leprosy.

Gehazi left the prophet's presence white as snow and disappeared into the ranks of the forgotten, leaving behind only a forwarding address to a living hell. That is our final snapshot of the hotshot who tried to fool the prophet of God.

So how did his name end up on a royal VIP list? Why do we find him in the royal palace, reminiscing with the king of Israel like he was his long-lost buddy?

Aren't You Supposed to Be Hanging Out in Hell?

This man was a condemned felon. He was supposed to be hanging out in hell, not in a king's palace. It was part of his life sentence administered through the prophet Elisha (a prophet who was still very much alive).

If you were a leper in Jewish society in Elisha's day, then you were *not* going to enter the king's court. And you could just forget about entering the king's presence. You wouldn't even get past the city gate in most instances.

Remember, lepers were considered ritually unclean, and therefore *dead* in ancient Jewish societies. You would be treated like the walking dead, doomed to live out your disfigured existence in enforced isolation.

If you have leprosy, you are not going to be whispering in the ear of the king of Israel. There were laws against that sort of thing. "We must protect the king from catching leprosy. *No* whispering in the king's ear!"

It is generally understood that when you are proverbially sentenced to hell by the oracle of God, you *stay there.* Obviously, *something* happened to orchestrate Gehazi's escape from leprosy and his unhappy home in hell! How could a leper hang out with a king?

This just couldn't be Gehazi *the leper* sitting in the king's court talking with the king! I remember reading about King Azariah of Judah, who got leprosy because of disobedience. He was kicked out of his own palace because of his disease! The Bible says his son had to rule as regent in his place.[10]

If a king with leprosy gets kicked out, then a servant with leprosy will get kicked out for sure! But here he is—back from the brink! We had all but written him off.

Perhaps some have done the same to you.

Seven Years and Three Verses from a Comeback Miracle

Doesn't it seem a little strange to you that this mother and son duo shows up in Gehazi's life *before* he gets leprosy? Then they reappear *seven years and one famine later.* Just *three verses away* from the mysterious reappearance of Gehazi—evidently *after* he was cured of leprosy!

Exactly what happened to link their lives so closely? How can we explain this "coincidental" drop-in visit seven years to the day from the prophet's revelation and at the very *moment* Gehazi is rehearsing a story with that same mother and son as the main stars?

This marks the place where the Divine Author steps back in time to establish a digression in plot. God took us backward so He could tell the story forward to some mysterious divine conclusion.

In this case, God used three verses to send us back seven years. God sets up the scene for the arrival of mother and son at the "fullness of time." At the exact moment, *literally*, when the lips of the leper-turned-court-adviser completed the story of the miracle of the mother and her son, they suddenly walked into the king's court!

Remember that at least seven years have passed *since Gehazi last saw this woman and her son.*

I have some good news for you. I believe there can be a "fullness of time" for you! I believe your promises are pregnant and about to give birth!

Seven Years of Shrouded Mystery to Unravel

The due date for the delivery of God's promise came when *Gehazi* mysteriously resurfaced from the depths of leprosy with new life and fresh favor. Somehow this man went from serving the prophet to serving the king. We know that much, but there are at least seven years of shrouded mystery to unravel before we can connect the two points.

Whatever happened in his life during the unknown dark years somehow coincided with the lives of the Shunammite woman and her son. Something happened that was powerful enough to transport Gehazi from hobbling with lepers in earthly hell to hobnobbing with a king in the royal palace of Israel!

Somehow, sometime, during those dark days and years of hell on earth, God set the stage for Gehazi's miracle comeback. And this one looks like an ultimate turnaround of true biblical proportions. How did God do it?

It reminds me of another time and another mystery. On this occasion, everyone involved in the story was confident the condemned man was down for the count. He could never come back—all of the "i's" were *dotted*, all of the "t's" *crossed*.

The Pharisees, lawyers, and scribes knew their stuff—this Man had been convicted of blasphemy and turned over to the Roman executioners. His fate was sealed—and for good measure, they sealed His tomb too. But remember, the tomb can become the womb!

Hell Just Announced an Escape . . . He's Back!

Their dark accomplices in hell were confident too. Everything that could be done had been done. Their greatest enemy was now their greatest trophy. His body was wrapped in the grave and all hope of His kingdom coming was over. Then it happened.

Hell's broken gates and death's shattered grip announced an escape! And heaven announced, "He's back!"

No one knew how it happened or how He did it. But hell knew the party was over. Jesus was alive, again! He's back!

The words "He's back!" sum up what we know about Gehazi. It begs the question "How did Gehazi get 'back'?" How did he make such an ultimate and unlikely comeback? Is this kind of miracle turnaround available to everybody? Can you turn such a bad night into a good day?

CHAPTER 7

God Does His Best Work in Secret

You Can Turn a Bad Night Into a Good Day

Gehazi is an *enigma* (that's a fancy word for a mystery, a riddle, a puzzle).

We know what he was after walking out of Elisha's presence: a leper, cursed and condemned. We also know what he was apparently like when the Shunammite woman and her son showed up in the king's throne room: restored and an intimate with the king.

Gehazi obviously was *different* from the first instance to the second. No one could be in such close proximity and intimate conversation with the king and have leprosy.

So what happened to the judgment pronounced over Gehazi because of his sins? Was he pardoned? If so, who staged this turnaround and how was it done? Remember that Elisha, the oracle of God, declared, "Naaman's skin disease will now infect you and your family, *with no relief in sight*"![1]

That sounds permanent. Fatal. Terminal. Like a life sentence with no parole. A curse of biblical proportions. An incurable illness resulting in extreme disfigurement and progressive deterioration leading to painful death. Gehazi disappears into the darkness of leprosy and the fog of the forgotten people who seemingly "don't deserve to be remembered."

Did he hire a high-powered battery of attorneys skilled at

defending high-profile clients? Did he have a powerful relative high in government, or did some top government official commute his sentence? Who pulled strings to get his sentence commuted? All of these might have been possible if his accuser and judge were anyone but God.

How can we begin to explain the "mysterious path" of Gehazi's return? Could it be that his turnaround is similar in some way to other mysterious recoveries in God's Word?

During my search for answers to the life of Gehazi, the Lord seemed to bring a favorite biblical character into my mind—Esther.

A Mysterious Ability to Do His Best Work in Secret

On the night in Esther's life that everything approached its dramatic conclusion, God again revealed a mysterious ability to do His best work in secret.

Esther decided to take action against her enemy, Haman. She prepared an elaborate banquet for the king to set the stage for her petition. No doubt, she had expectation mixed with anxiety.

The Bible says, **"On that night . . ."**[2]

Have you ever had such a "bad" night that you could always and forever reference it by the simple phrase *"that night"*? Well, *"that night"* for Esther was really bad. It was bad because she had hoped and planned for a resolution to her problem; she had gained access to the king, created the atmosphere, and at the end of the night, *her circumstances had not changed.*

Perhaps you've watched as circumstances continue to align themselves against you on your job, in your marriage, with your children, or in your finances. You did everything you know to do—you went to church, you prayed, you even knelt at the altar and stayed longer than anyone else. You gave more in the offering, you fasted, and you did everything you felt you needed to do, but your circumstances did not change. The impending doom of what was about to happen hung heavy over you.

Faith is not really tested during a worship service while you are in the presence of the King. Your faith will be tested *after* the service. It's what you do *after* church, *after* salvation, *after* you've done everything and apparently nothing has changed.

In Esther's situation, *after* she risked her life to enter the presence of the king unbidden, her enemy still existed—his powers intact, his plans proceeding. He was ready to execute legalized murder against every Jewish person in the Persian Empire.

This is how I know this was a bad night for Esther. The first banquet concluded with seemingly nothing accomplished. I believe she was totally aware that her enemy's plans were proceeding. She knew the king was unaware of the dire straits she and her uncle faced if Haman's plot to eradicate the Jews succeeded.

Despite all of Esther's efforts (short of revealing her secret identity to the king), nothing worked; so Esther invited the king and Haman to another banquet the following night. But nothing worked in Esther's favor! The night was over and all that could be done was to make plans for another night. All of Esther's plans seemed to be of no avail. It was going to be a *very* bad night.

When they all went home after that final night's banquet, I don't think *any* of them slept. The Bible states definitely, "On that night could not the king sleep."[3]

Up All Night Constructing an Instrument of Execution

We infer that Haman didn't sleep because, at the urging of his wife and friends, he decided to seek permission from King Xerxes the next morning to execute Mordecai the Jew so he could go and be happy the evening of Esther's second banquet.[4]

So intense was his hatred toward Mordecai that Haman apparently stayed up all night on *"that night"* to construct an instrument of execution for Esther's adopted father. That way it would be ready and waiting for action *before* Haman's early morning visit to petition the king for the execution.[5]

Meanwhile, Esther was gripped with heartbreaking secrets she could not reveal to anyone before the proper time. She wrestled with the anxious knowledge that no decision was being made and no action had been taken to save her people. The jury was still out; in fact, the petition had not even been presented yet!

(Have you ever had one of those days when you felt totally exasperated because key events had been taken completely out of your control or influence? You want to shout in protest, "Wait! I didn't even get to have my say!")

In the small enclave of the women's quarters in the royal palace, construction noises would carry far enough for Esther to hear the echoes of Haman's midnight work crew. Although the Scriptures do not confirm it, I believe that Esther *suspected* Mordecai was the intended victim for Haman's homicidal whims (she'd always had good and trusted relationships with the king's eunuchs, who seemed to see and hear everything).

Imagine how difficult it would be for Queen Esther to fall asleep while being forced to listen to the racket of pounding hammers and rasping saws. Could it be that she was literally *listening* to her enemy build an instrument of execution for Mordecai, her adopted father, the man who had raised and nurtured her from childhood?

While Esther tossed and turned, alternating between prayers of desperation and unsuccessful attempts at sleep, Haman happily engineered the demise of Mordecai. Meanwhile, the Bible tells us, "On that night could not the king sleep."[6]

Perhaps to help him overcome his divine insomnia, the king asked for someone to read the court records to him. (If anything should put you to sleep, it would be the reading of court records.)

The servant droned on and on while Persia's supreme monarch stared at the ceiling. Suddenly his attention was jarred by a paragraph describing the deeds of a royal scribe named Mordecai. This man had learned of a plot to assassinate the king hatched by two of his own royal chamberlains, "the keepers of the door." (Today we call them personal bodyguards.)

Mordecai had reported the news to Queen Esther and she certified the informant's validity and had it entered into the royal diary.

After an investigation confirmed the plot, the plotters were hung on a gallows.[7]

The king was pleased to be reminded of such a great service to the throne, but suddenly he sat upright in bed when the servant abruptly moved on to the next record. This was *not* the royal way of Persian kings. Surely this record was not finished!

"What honor and dignity hath been done to Mordecai for this?" the king asked. When he learned that nothing had been done, the king acted immediately.[8]

What an interesting discovery! What do kings do when they can't sleep? *They check the records.*

Reward delayed is not reward denied.

You may be enduring a bad night or perhaps a bad week, my friend, but take heart. Just because you are enduring a sleepless season, that doesn't mean we have a snoring King. The Bible says, "Behold, he that keepeth Israel shall neither slumber nor sleep."[9] When you face a "that night" crisis that robs you of sleep, remember that your King is fully awake as well.

And what do kings do when they cannot sleep? They check the records. Reward delayed is not reward denied.

While Esther tossed and turned, her king checked the records and discovered Mordecai's good deed. The next thing we know, the king was no longer checking the records, he had shifted his focus to planning Mordecai's reward!

What happened when Haman's plans collided with the king's plans? Often what the king plans in private is revealed in public. Circumstances prevented Esther from knowing what the king had been planning all night. All she knew was that the Jewish people had a death sentence hovering over them, and there seemed to be little hope anything would improve after the events of "that night."

As a resident of Louisiana, I remember a night like that. In the fall of 2005, I breathed a personal sigh of relief when Hurricane Katrina skirted our city. While my friends to the south were decimated by

Hurricane Katrina, our city was the first major city north of the line of devastation that never lost power.

My sigh of relief was short-lived. Only a few short weeks later, Katrina's wicked twin sister, Hurricane Rita, visited our state. On this occasion, her aim was a little more to the west and her reach extended farther inland. I remember "that night" when Hurricane Rita hit my house.

I watched as the hurricane hit—not someone else's home, but—my home!

It's one thing to watch, through the small window of a television, the devastation being wreaked on other people's homes. But when the hurricane hits *your house*, then your bedroom window replaces the "electronic window"! Before long, I'd abandoned the television and found myself standing at my bedroom window. (The TV had become useless as a window to the outside world because all electricity was lost.)

Then my gaze permanently shifted to the window on the front of my house, and *I watched as the hurricane hit—not someone else's home, but—my home!* I quietly reassured my family. They all stayed awake as long as their bodies would allow.

My daughters were tucked in after much initial reassurance. When the electricity went off, they awakened and I quickly shushed them and told them, again, that I believed everything was going to be okay.

I don't know if that was my faith speaking, or the voice of a father trying to calm his family. I wasn't sure everything was going to be okay, and in fact, I didn't sleep at all "that" night. I went from window to window, watching as limbs crashed and debris flew through the streets. The temperature began to rise in the house as we had no electricity to power the air conditioner.

My fear also began to rise. I had seen what a hurricane can do. I knew we were all in for a long, bad night.

Storms Can Leave You Weak and Dry

About the time the sun began to come up, the winds began to subside. My exhaustion forced me into a restless sleep. We had survived.

We had no power and no water, but we were alive. Sometimes storms do that to you. They leave you powerless and dry. For some of you, the important fact right now is a very simple one:

You are still here.

Satan may have tried to take you out, you may be in a weakened condition, *but you're still here!*

Even after the storm passed, the problem was not completely gone. Hurricanes leave deep footprints that often take a long time to erase.

For Esther, the name of her hurricane was Haman. For me, the name of my hurricane that night was Rita. I don't know the name of your hurricane. It could be depression, or divorce, or cancer, or the loss caused by unexpected job layoffs.

The storm was so big for Esther on "that night" that simply waiting out the terror just wasn't enough. Even after Esther prayed, Haman's plans continued. The hammers pounded, and the saws buzzed as evil plans continued.

What If the Instrument of Your Demise Will Be Finished Tomorrow?

It's as if you see the proverbial handwriting on the wall that the construction of the enemy's instrument of your demise will be finished tomorrow. If tonight is a "bad night," then tomorrow looks to be a "worse day"!

What Esther did not know was though Haman might not have been sleeping, *neither was the king.* "On that night could not the king sleep . . ." Even as Haman happily engineered Mordecai's execution, a sleepless king checked the records and discovered Mordecai's good deeds.

God always checks the records and he always plans a reward. Remember, when Haman's plans collide with the king's plans, then what the king has planned in private often is revealed in public.

The secret plans of the palace trumped the public construction of Haman's gallows. "That *night* . . ." is not the end of the story.

Esther 6:1 begins with, "On that *night* . . ."

But Esther 8:1 begins with, "On that *day* . . ."

It is not always a bad night, it just often seems like a bad night. A bad night can turn into a good day *if faith has not wavered*. You may feel as if you've been going through a bad week or a bad month, but remember: Your King is still awake! "Weeping may endure for a night, but joy cometh in the morning"![10]

Now let's talk about *the potential of what can happen on a "good day."*

The king's private planning would publicly collide with Haman's early the next morning. With the gallows complete and his family planning his victory celebration at home, Haman was the *first official* to troop into the outer court of the king, hoping to catch the king's ear before the lesser citizens could clutter the day—he had an execution to attend to.

Obviously the king was still awake and contemplating Mordecai's reward when Haman appeared to ask for Mordecai's neck—literally. When the king's servant announced the first arrival in the court, the king immediately invited Haman into the inner court where, according to the Bible, Mordecai's accuser was asked a question (and framed his own answer):

> "What shall be done for the man whom the king delights to honor?" Now Haman thought in his heart, "Whom would the king delight to honor more than me?"[11]

Haman couldn't believe it, he had been given "carte blanche" to create his own dream day. As we read this, we discover that Haman's response was to call for the king's royal robe, the king's own horse, and "the crown royal which is set upon his head."[12] That wasn't enough. Haman had more!

> Then let this robe and horse be delivered to the hand of one of the king's most noble princes, that he may array *the man* whom the king delights to honor. Then

parade him on horseback through the city square, and proclaim before him: "Thus shall it be done to *the man* whom the king delights to honor!"[13]

Even the most thinly veiled reading gives us a peek into the giant ego of Haman—*he wanted to be king!* His secret lust for public honor and royal acclaim was showing. He thought this was about *him!* He arrogantly walked into the king's court to make an accusation, and he was asked a question. *Sometimes our ego can write a check that our character cannot cash.*

Haman had begun "that day" with high hopes. First he would enjoy an unexpected and unmatched royal parade given in his honor that morning. His afternoon schedule was blocked off for a long-awaited vengeful murder of hated Mordecai. That would be followed by a prescheduled exclusive evening audience and banquet with the king and queen.

Then Haman's plans collided head-on with the king's plans and things changed—*permanently.* The royal agenda was about to go *very* public.

Can you imagine the scene? Just as Haman started to say, "Now, Your Majesty, *about Mor*—," he received an abrupt interruption from the king. This sleep-deprived monarch had a royal recognition to attend to.

Having heard Haman's dream plan, the king replied, "That is an excellent idea!"

"*Haman, get my horse . . .*"

I visualize Haman inwardly chuckling at his good fortune.

"*And get my robe and crown. Do all that you have said . . .*"

Haman tucks his head in false modesty as he sucks in his breath in anticipation of being so honored.

"*. . . to* **Mordecai**, *who sits in the gate.*"

I wish that you and I could have been there on that day to watch Haman's crestfallen face as he realized he was not the object of this grand scheme of self-promotion—but Mordecai was!

Then the king quickly followed up, saying, "And Haman, I can think of no better dignitary to lead Mordecai through the streets of the city *than you*." What Haman thought would be a good day in which his enemy was executed, became Haman's bad day.

What Esther, and perhaps Mordecai, thought would be a bad day, became a good day as Mordecai was elevated and Haman was deflated and crushed![14]

In one night, "the man whom Haman plotteth to kill" had become "the man whom the king delighteth to honor." Ancient wisdom has always dictated that when a man is a friend of a king, then his enemies become the king's enemies. The value of Haman's political stock was crashing through the floor. This was the beginning of Haman's end, and the end of Esther and Mordecai's beginning.

Haman's bad day was about to get much, *much* worse. Not only had he found himself on the south end of the king's honor roll, but he had that small problem of a towering gallows in his yard—the one he had built for Mordecai.

After the parade, Mordecai returned in unprecedented honor to the king's gate. Haman, on the other hand, covered his head in shame and returned to his front door as if he was in a funeral procession. Just as he finished canceling his celebration party and bemoaning his sorrow to shocked family and friends, the king's bodyguards arrived to personally escort the bleary-eyed official to the banquet with the queen. This was the banquet he had planned to attend happily, unencumbered by Mordecai's continued existence.

First, the execution had turned into a parade. Now the banquet would turn into a charade. Perhaps Haman had hopes that he might still manage to salvage his drooping career as he gazed at the king and the lovely queen. He may even have comforted himself over his "bad day" with the statement "At least *they* still like me . . ."

When the queen's guests were fully satisfied with her banquet fare, the king asked Queen Esther once again to tell him what she would not reveal the night before, "What is your petition?" Neither the king nor Haman were prepared for her answer.

After following the usual court protocols for formal address, Queen Esther said:

> If it pleases the king, let my life be given me at my petition, and my people at my request.
>
> For we have been sold, my people and I, to be destroyed, to be killed, and to be annihilated. Had we been sold as male and female slaves, I would have held my tongue, although the enemy could never compensate for the king's loss.[15]

Haman wanted to be *anywhere else* but in that private audience in that moment. His "good night" had really begun to look like his worst nightmare.

One of the most powerful earthly kings in history was angry and he was looking for a good target! Haman wanted to be very small in that moment, but his giant ego made it impossible to hide. "Who is he, and where is he, who would dare presume in his heart to do such a thing?" the king thundered.[16]

This was Esther's moment. Her good day had spilled over into an exceptionally good night!

> And Esther said, "The adversary and enemy is this wicked Haman!" So Haman was terrified before the king and queen.[17]

When Esther pointed to Haman, the king grew so angry that he had to leave the room . . . and he looked for his bodyguards in the meantime.

Haman moved over to Esther's reclining coach, draped himself across it, and began blubbering for mercy on Esther's sleeve—just as the king returned with his guards! "Will he also assault the queen while I am in the house?" the king exclaimed, and the royal bodyguards instantly covered Haman's head with a sack.[18]

Only the night before, Haman had planned to *solve his problems* by hanging Mordecai on a specially built gallows in his own backyard.

But on *that night*, the king's bodyguard mentioned the gallows to the king and explained that it was built for Mordecai's execution, so the king used Haman's instrument of execution to *solve his problem*. He ordered that Haman be hung in his own backyard on the same specially built gallows he'd personally designed for Mordecai.

We are *still* talking about the potential of what can happen on a "good day." When the King's plans trump the enemy's plans for your life, *anything* can happen!

> On *that day* did the king Ahasuerus [Xerxes] give the house of Haman the Jews' enemy unto Esther the queen . . .
>
> And the king took off his ring, which he had taken from Haman, and gave it unto Mordecai. And Esther set Mordecai over the house of Haman.[19]

Haman spent a lifetime—even if it turned out to be a short one—accumulating wealth, possessions, and land. *In one moment*, at the king's command, *everything* evil Haman owned transferred to Esther. Then Esther delivered control of all Haman's hoarded wealth to his most hated enemy—Mordecai.

In biblical terms of reference, that included his whole household—every camel, every cow, every sheep, every manservant, every maidservant. If Haman had a mountain cabin, it was now Mordecai's. The mansion and estate? The beach house? The cars and the yacht? The Swiss bank account? *All Mordecai's.*

Sometimes we grow depressed watching our enemy accumulate things, but could it be that *according to the King's plans*, the enemy is not accumulating for himself? What if he is simply accumulating and taking care of *your things* until it is *your turn*?

The secret plans of the king caused a divine reversal of fortune that allowed Esther's family and Mordecai to rise to an unprecedented place of prominence and provision. Esther's bad night turned into a good day. In fact, the process was already working while she was worrying!

If you had asked Esther on "that night" how things were going, she would have said, "Very badly." What she didn't know was that the King does his best work in secret. What you may not know is while you are trying to survive, God's secret plan for you is to thrive!

On Esther's darkest night, divine insomnia overtook a powerful monarch and led him to review the royal records and plan a royal restitution in Mordecai's honor. The dark of night often matches those dark nights of the soul we all experience in life, the seasons when hope seems lost and we fear the sun will never rise for us again.

God Works the Night Shift

For Esther and the countless Jews living under the power of the Persian Empire on "that night," things looked bad, as if it were the beginning of the end. As they discovered the following day, *God works the night shift.*

We are talking about a God who can create the worlds in one day. Just imagine what might happen if He were to stay up all night? He crafts comebacks and miraculous turnarounds even while we toss and turn in despair over our circumstances. God has the final say, and He does His best work in *secret.*

Even if you have 20/20 vision, you cannot see what is going on in heaven's throne room. You can't see into the dark unknown. But God has "29/29 vision"! We read in Deuteronomy **29:29**:

> The *secret things* belong to the LORD our God, but those things *which are revealed* belong to us and to our children forever . . .[20]

God can work in the dark—in fact He does His best work in our darkest times. Surely He can change your "bad night" into a good day—He did it for Esther. He will do it for you! Remember how

Esther chapter 8 begins with the words, "On that day . . ."? One of the *last* verses of chapter 8 of Esther states: "The Jews had joy and gladness, a feast and a ***good day***"![21]

Did you read that? "A *good day*." Now let's go write the end of *your* story.

Samson's Story Can Be Your Story

Do you remember Samson's story? He was the man whose reputation was restored enough to be placed in the Book of Hebrew's Hall of Faith. That story provides another proof of God's secret restorative work in the background. Samson had all of the outward characteristics of a hero and leader. He started his career spectacularly and regularly humiliated his enemies, the Philistines. He made mockery of their best warriors and most elaborate plots to entrap him.

Yet, from God's viewpoint, Samson was outwardly strong but inwardly weak. Outward strength wasn't enough; He wanted to restore Samson's inward man.

When your outward talent is greater than your inward character, there is often a crash. Samson's crash was spectacular, but so was his restoration. We learn from his story that God restores the "inward man" *before* there is outward evidence.

Samson Was a He-Man with a She-Weakness

Samson's weakness of character betrayed his God-given gift and derailed his spiritual calling. He dismissed God's warnings and freely crossed boundaries of safety and propriety. When Delilah betrayed him and cut off the seven locks of his long hair, it caused him to fall into the cruel hands of his enemies.

By some accounts, Delilah means "delicate." I should add, "delicate, *but dangerous*." Samson was a he-man with a she-weakness. He could not be brought down by a man's strong hands, but he was trapped by the "weak" hands of a woman.

Blinded, humiliated, and bound to a prison-house grinding wheel with chains of bronze, Samson crushed grain like a working ox as a national trophy and prized public spectacle. Living in his own personal darkness, he looked more like some twisted zoo exhibit than a mighty judge of Israel.[22] (Sin has a blinding, binding, grinding effect; and Delilah's scissors are still sharp!)

Samson sinned against God, he failed his nation, and he brought disrespect to his family. Now, day after day, even the lowest specimens of Philistine culture taunted and mocked the blind captive without fear.

Samson's Grow-Back Triggered His Comeback!

Unknown to his overconfident captors, the God who does His best work in secret heard Samson's humble cries of repentance. A surprise comeback had already been launched from heaven the day that hair began to grow back on the head of Israel's Nazarite champion. *Samson's grow-back triggered his comeback!* What was once dead in your soul *can* grow back.

The Philistines foolishly forgot that only after they shaved Samson's seven braids of hair did they gain the upper hand. They didn't notice Samson's hair was growing back, *but God did*—and He never forgets His promises.

As Samson's hair grew longer and time grew shorter, a surprise comeback was rising underneath the Philistines' noses. Samson's inner man was growing stronger than the outer man.

Finally, on what looked to be the worst day of a long unbroken string of bad days, Samson cried out to God in repentance. Three thousand Philistines gathered for a great feast, and blind Samson was the entertainment.

In their excitement, the Philistines called for Samson to be moved from his place at the prison-house grinding wheel to a prominent place between the two central pillars of their meeting place. The assembled lords and leaders of Philistia made Samson entertain them, and they began to mock him and revel in their abuse of this once-feared Israelite warrior.

His internal *desire became* external *strength with* eternal *consequence.*

Perhaps no one but God noticed that when the Philistines chained Samson into position between the pillars, their old enemy looked much as he did in his heyday of power. Blind but with his hair now fully grown, Samson had rededicated himself to the Lord. The stage was now set for a comeback!

When Samson said, "Let me *feel* the pillars . . . ,"[23] the internal desire became external strength with eternal consequence. You have to *feel it* internally before you can do it externally.

While others may have given up and assumed that "*what had been*" would define "*what would be*," Samson prayed a prayer of faith and humble desperation. After living a life of self-absorption and self-gratification, Samson was now totally focused on destroying the enemies of his people. If it cost him his life, it meant nothing.

It reminds me of something someone else said one time, someone who became a champion of God: "For to me, to live is Christ, and to die is gain."[24]

The Judge Who Failed Prayed a Comeback Prayer

Samson, who had been a judge over Israel, asked the young Philistine who guided him to let him lean against the support pillars of the arena with his hands so he could rest. Then Samson prayed a selfless comeback prayer, asking God to look on him again, and to give him supernatural strength once more: "O Lord GOD, remember me, I pray! Strengthen me, I pray . . ."[25]

Then Samson extended his scarred arms to the left and to the right until he was able to press his thickly calloused palms against the two stone pillars supporting the roof of the crowded building.

Taking a deep breath, he began to push outward—pressing with supernatural force against the rough-hewn pillars as if shoving aside years of failure. Empowered by the God who does His best restoration work in secret, this judge of Israel was about to deliver a final judgment on his enemies. Under their noses he had been restored!

> Saying, "Let me die with the Philistines," Samson pushed hard with all his might. The building crashed on the tyrants and all the people in it. He killed more people in his death than he had killed in his life.[26]

The fact is that Israel had *fewer* enemies and *more* freedom on "that day" than at any point under Samson's leadership as a judge over his nation.[27] He had been restored!

As remarkable as Samson's story may be, Lazarus "the friend of Jesus" may be the *least likely* "comeback kid" of the Scriptures. This nearly invisible New Testament character was minding his own business, living in relative obscurity with his two bickering sisters, when suddenly he found himself thrust into crisis.

The name of Lazarus has become a byword and symbol of the ultimate "comeback"! I know we discussed his comeback earlier, but there is no better comeback story than his. After all, he "came back" from the dead!

Rehearsing the Words That Jesus Shouted

In countless tongues and cultural settings, preachers, teachers, and people in trouble have rehearsed the words that Jesus shouted at the tomb imprisoning Lazarus's cold body: "Lazarus, come forth!"[28]

With the shout that shook hell and robbed the grave, Jesus rescued His friend from death and gave early notice that a visitor was coming to hell itself. Lazarus was a common name at that time. But a *rhema* word kept every other buried Lazarus in Israel from coming out of the tomb. When the Logos speaks a rhema,[29] He gets specific: "This is for you, Lazarus." This book may be a resurrection word for just one person—*you*.

Think of the impact of the Lord's command in terms of "one

buried grain of wheat named Lazarus." He spoke to that one grain of wheat. *I* can't speak for everybody, but He *can* speak to you!

John Mark is another man who came back from miserable failure. We know how he failed early in the Book of Acts and how he was rejected as unworthy for missionary service by one of the church's most respected and powerful missionaries.

How Do You Return from the Dead Zone of Failure?

What we *don't know* is how John Mark returned from the "dead zone" of failure. How was he named as one of the only faithful men to stand by the same man who had rejected him—at the end of that apostle's life?

John Mark failed miserably as a member of his uncle's ministry team early in church history. He was chosen to accompany Barnabas and Paul on their first ministry trip, but "chickened" out and quit the team under the pressures and challenges of the mission field. He abandoned Barnabas and Paul and returned home alone early; leaving the two apostles to forge on without him.[30]

(Don't the Scriptures say something about one who puts his hand to the plow and looks back?[31])

The apostles completed their journey with historic results and ultimately returned home. Some time later, while planning another major apostolic trip to Gentile lands, Barnabas wanted to take along John Mark again, but Paul wouldn't have it.

John Mark's failure made such a deep mark on Paul the Apostle that he *refused* to take the guy on the trip, even if it meant he had to go *without* Barnabas! John Mark hadn't merely failed; he had dug his own grave and climbed in.

> Barnabas wanted to take John along, the John nick-named Mark. But Paul wouldn't have him; he wasn't about to take along a quitter who, as soon as the going got tough, had jumped ship on them in Pamphylia. Tempers flared, and they ended up going their separate

ways: Barnabas took Mark and sailed for Cyprus; Paul chose Silas and .. went to Syria and Cilicia.[32]

Paul's Distrust of John Mark Seemed Permanent

It is clear to us how and where John Mark failed. Paul's distrust of the nephew of Barnabas is unmistakable—even with the passage of time. Anyone looking on would say it was *permanent*. (And it appears that up to that point, John Mark had given no evidence that anything had changed.)

Sometimes what you need is a loved one who won't turn loose. It was a loved one named Barnabas (the son of consolation) who "couldn't turn loose of a failure" that contributed to John Mark's turnaround. They just can't let you drown in the sea of your own mistakes.

So at the very end of Paul's life, it was to John Mark that he appealed. Once again, we do *not* know what happened in the hidden years between John Mark's failure and his faithful stand with Paul at the end of his ministry. Yet something *had* to have happened to change a failure into a success, a coward into a hero. In a letter to his disciple and apostle in training, Timothy, Paul wrote:

> Get here as fast as you can. Demas, chasing fads, went off to Thessalonica and left me here. Crescens is in Galatia province, Titus in Dalmatia. Luke is the only one here with me. *Bring Mark with you; he'll be my right-hand man* [he is *profitable to me for the ministry* (KJV)].[33]

In the beginning, John Mark couldn't even handle the temporary rigors of travel. At the end, Mark stood firm with Paul—even in the face of official disapproval and persecution from Rome and Jerusalem.

All it takes is one brief instance of repentance, a single slight turn of the heart, and God floods the scene with unseen comeback power. The presence of God can change everything.

All of these stories are good, but that still doesn't tell us how our main character, Gehazi, shows up again, apparently restored.

Why do we probe so hard to understand this turnaround mystery? Perhaps it is to give all of us hope that somehow—in some unforeseen way—a restoration can come to our own lives. Do you need restoration somewhere in your life?

Wouldn't you like to see a tsunami of restoration transform your situation so completely that everybody will notice the change? Would you like to hear people say, "The last time I saw you, things weren't going so well. Just look at you now! Tell me, how did this happen?"

That might not be you now; you may still be "in the dark." If so, take heart. When God gets ready to restore, He does His best work in the dark!

Let me give you an example. When God was ready to do the work of redemption at the cross, He flicked the "off" switch on the sun and caused darkness to come on the earth.[34] It was as if He was saying, "What I am about to do is so incredible, that you will never understand it or properly handle it without My help. So I am just going to turn out the lights." (He turns out the lights so no one can say, "I saw it all, I understand everything.")

At this point, all I can tell you again is that sometimes God does His best work in secret. When you are in a prison of despair, God is often setting the stage for a pardon! You just don't know it. And others might not know it either.

Perhaps you know what it is like to be living in isolation, just trying to survive in the wilderness of failure, in the desert place of unendurable pain and hurt. Then it happens; somehow, you don't know exactly what or how it happened, but suddenly you are on the path to restoration!

Have Your Mistakes Put You Under a Curse?

You may feel you've made such serious mistakes in your own life that you are living under a curse permanently. If God can restore Gehazi, then He can restore you! But let me warn you: *Don't you let your past dictate your future.*

Gehazi had seven years to relive each detail of his life. He must have struggled to keep life in his limbs and hope in his heart. It is almost guaranteed that he scratched incessantly at his itching body.

Imagine spending nearly eighty long months rehearsing every step he took in his sad downward journey from a life of blessing to life under a terminal curse.

Don't you let your past dictate your future.

Can you conceive of the sorrow Gehazi endured in those long pain-filled nights? Every hidden motive leading to his downfall haunted his dreams. Every waking thought was filled with the loneliness of his cursed existence!

He believed he was living a nightmare of sorrow that could only end in death and darkness, yet there was a learning process going on.

Gehazi was taught the lesson, *but he didn't listen!* He was taught the lesson about the power of repentance when the leprosy of Naaman was taken away. Naaman repented of his arrogance, went, dipped, and was made whole.

Could it be that Gehazi spent seven years in contrition and repentance because he didn't learn "the lesson of seven dips"?

Finally, he said, "God did it for Naaman. He can do it for me." It took Naaman seven dips. It took Gehazi seven years. Naaman's quick restoration probably befuddled and angered Gehazi. "Why" is most often "Why not now?" Be patient. Make good choices. Don't focus on how long you wandered in the wilderness. Focus on the promise of restoration. You will come full circle. The river Jordan awaits. You'll get to take the test again.

Don't get caught up in the timeline of your recovery—focus on obedience. Some people recover so quickly that we might call them "seven-dip wonders." Don't trip over the snare of jealousy, rejoice with them and learn from their lessons.

Perhaps you feel more like the people who recover slowly—sometimes you wonder if you will *ever* break free! Allow God to have His way. Recovery is in the making—whether or not you can explain it or accurately anticipate its arrival.

Because we are allowed to peek through the window of the Scriptures to see "the end from the beginning" in Gehazi's life, we know that somehow God would prepare this prophet's ex-servant for an undeserved and unexpected second chance.

Gehazi is about to become our "poster boy" for hope and restoration. If he can come back, then so can you! Perhaps his life will become your road map for the way back!

God knows how to change and transform modern Gehazis in preparation for an improbable comeback.

Most of how it happened in Gehazi's life is a secret. We simply don't know how. We just know it happened! Gehazi experienced the ultimate comeback. But perhaps we can make some "guesstimates" as to how it happened.

Could it be . . . ?

CHAPTER 8

Uh-Oh . . . I've Got a Bad Feeling About This
"We Do Not Well . . ."

Seven years after being covered with leprosy and condemned to its bitter death along with his sons, Gehazi appears again, very much alive. His body is intact. The leprosy has obviously and mysteriously disappeared, and this outcast is now a very prominent and favored insider.

From outside the city to inside the court. What could possibly explain such a miracle, a come-from-behind turnaround? (You can probably imagine some of my thought process as I studied the Scriptures.)

> I know Gehazi became a leper along with his sons. I watched him disappear from the pages of the Bible record . . . he just isn't there—anywhere.
>
> But then this guy shows up again three chapters later—in the presence of Israel's king and apparently without any sign of leprosy.
>
> God, that's good and that's great, but give me some clue, how did You do that? This guy was bad. He was stealing money, lying, and making up stories to manipulate offerings from grateful people!
>
> We are talking about an abuse of power at the highest level! God, how could You restore somebody like that? He was cursed,

and he deserved it! He was a living dead man, and so were his sons.

We see Gehazi's name eight times before he decided to follow Naaman's gold. Then he is named when he lied to the prophet Elisha, just before he was cursed with leprosy for life.[1] The last two times Gehazi shows up he is with the king![2] But there is no sign of Gehazi in between these events—not a single mention of his name. Hmmm . . .

Well, maybe the Bible doesn't refer to him by name. Maybe it just talks about something that would mark his identity.

Now Gehazi was a leper. Leprosy may show up somewhere in the Bible narrative. Leprosy, lepers, leper . . . Is there any place in the Bible, between Gehazi's curse and his showing up in the throne room, that references leprosy?

Now I Must Get Theological and Theoretical

The only references I found in the narrative that referred to lepers or leprosy were two mentions in Second Kings chapter 7.[3]

> Now there were four leprous men at the entrance of the gate; and they said to one another, "Why are we sitting here until we die?
>
> "If we say, 'We will enter the city,' the famine is in the city, and we shall die there. And if we sit here, we die also."[4]

Did you notice the word "leprous"?

I found this curious passage in Second Kings, sandwiched between Gehazi's ignominious exit and his grand reappearance.

Does this mention of leprosy connect to Gehazi? Is it possible? Is it provable? Who are these lepers sitting by the gate? What happened to them?

We know Gehazi was restored, but the truth of the matter is that we just don't know how he was restored. The Bible does not spell out *how* it happened; only *that* it happened.

The only thing we know is that the last time we see Gehazi in Second Kings 5:27, he was a "dead duck." He had full-blown leprosy, his future had been aborted, his marriage probably over, his finances for sure in the tank.

Then the next time Gehazi shows up, he is buddy-buddy with the king of Israel. So here we are, thousands of years later, asking ourselves, "How did it happen?"

What famine are these lepers talking about? Could this be the famine that the prophet spoke of to the Shunammite woman? It is in the right place. Elisha told her, "Take your family and move to some other place, for the LORD has called for a *famine on Israel that will last for seven years.*"[5]

That would explain why somewhere near the end of that seven-year famine, we find these four lepers sitting outside the city gate of Samaria debating among themselves, "If we go in the city we'll die there, but if we sit here, we'll die here."

As if seven long years of near-starvation and lack weren't enough, Syria returned to its old tricks and launched a military siege of Samaria. By surrounding the city and shutting off what little food was making its way to the people, the siege produced a situation that was unbearable.

By this time, even the "normal" people *inside* the fortified city were starving. If the desperation and hunger inside the walls were out of control, then outcast lepers who lived *outside* the walls were really in trouble.

Sometimes life gets so difficult that you feel as if you are on life support . . .

In the best of times, they survived on the trash thrown outside the city, with supplemental food left by family members or other generous people inside the city. These were terrible times—even the trash had become too precious to discard.

According to the Bible, food was so scarce that people were

paying two pounds of silver for a donkey's head—you read it correctly—a *donkey's head*![6] Can you imagine that?

Sometimes life gets so difficult that you feel as if you are on life support. Even the slightest problem or power outage could create a life crisis. If a person is literally on life support, then it's all over for them if power is interrupted for just a few moments.

This was *worse* than merely "life as normal" for the four lepers. They were at the bottom of the Samarian food chain—if the city was operating at the edge of total starvation, then hands-down the outcast lepers were the ones most likely to die during the famine. When "normal" people started depleting the city trash supply for survival, they essentially confiscated the lepers' primary food supply.

One Cup of Dove's Dung, Please

It gets worse. People were even paying two ounces of silver for a cup of *dove's dung*! What a combination: a donkey's head and dove's dung! (What do you do with a cup of dove's dung? My guess is that these desperate city dwellers hoped to harvest some undigested grain from the excrement of doves. Now that is *desperation*.)

This sounds like a meal scavenged from ancient "Dumpster diving." Yet, things got even *worse*!

Hand-wringing and worry escalated when the king of Israel talked with a woman of the city about her problem of coming up with the next meal in her house . . .

> This woman came to me and said, "Give up your son and we'll have him for today's supper; tomorrow we'll eat my son." So we cooked my son and ate him. The next day I told her, "Your turn—bring your son so we can have him for supper." But she had hidden her son away.[7]

The king was nearly beside himself with anger and frustration! He must have been wondering, "What *else* could go wrong?"

Top Kid Consumers

Our modern society also eats its kids—it just does it in different and more subtle ways.

- The selfish pop culture chews them up and spits them out—kids are seen more as prey, viable target markets and core consumers, than as impressionable children.
- Illicit drugs and sex consume children at earlier ages because our pleasure-worshipping society aggressively promotes the pursuit of emotional and physical "highs" at any cost—*and any age.*
- We pull down the "walls" of our own homes with parenting styles that put jobs, hobbies, and our personal comfort ahead of caring for and nurturing our children.
- Legalized abortion moves the child "eating" process to the earliest possible stage.

Do you understand how upside down their value system had become? Normally, mothers would sacrifice themselves in order for their children to survive. Now they were sacrificing their children to ensure their own survival.

You know a society is in trouble when it reaches this level. Is there hope? If it was this bad inside the city, imagine what it was like outside!

Four *other people* were facing just such impossible circumstances. With the scarred and barred main gate of Samaria behind them, and the sun setting over the camp of the invading Syrian army—their minds wrestled with desperate choices.

> It happened that four lepers were sitting just outside the city gate. They said to one another, "What are we doing sitting here at death's door? If we enter the famine-struck city we'll die; if we stay here we'll die. So let's take our chances in the camp of Aram [Syria]

and throw ourselves on their mercy. If they receive us we'll live, if they kill us we'll die. *We've got nothing to lose.*"[8]

These four lepers were caught between the proverbial "rock and a hard place." They were doomed if they stayed where they were, and they were doomed if they entered a city that had already banned them in good times—let alone in desperate times like these. So the prospect of doom with the Syrians didn't look so bad—at least there was a slim chance they might eat before they died a quick death.

Their decision was almost like this: "Let's get it over with. Let's not prolong the misery." It was Esther-like. You can almost hear the lepers whisper to one another in resigned voices, "If I perish, I perish."

> **When you are down to nothing, God is up to something!**

Sometimes circumstances move you to a place where any way you go it looks like you lose. It makes sense that these four lepers would end their joint tactical conference with the statement "*We've got nothing to lose.*"

God may also leave you at times with no choice but the right choice. *When you are down to nothing, God is up to something!*

Decision made, the sun went down, those four lepers gathered their tattered robes together, rearranged the bloody bandages on their disease-ravaged feet, and started their unsteady march toward the enemy camp.

Looking for Someone with Nothing to Lose

The siege had raged for some time. I wonder how long God had been looking for someone to start that march toward the enemy? Perhaps He tried to get the rebellious king to initiate action. Maybe He tried to persuade an Israelite army general to march on the enemy. This much seems likely—God knew it would take *somebody who had nothing to lose.*

What an attitude! Nothing to lose! Unconcerned about reputation. No money accumulated so there is none at risk. Health gone, no need to be cautious. In short, these lepers had nothing to lose. That's the hidden advantage of being "down and out"! There are no cautious self-serving, self-preserving actions at this point.

You are most dangerous when you have nothing to lose!

Ironically, *you are most dangerous when you have nothing to lose!* "For whoever desires to save his life will lose it, but whoever loses his life for My sake will save it."[9]

As long as you feel you have something to lose, you will battle misplaced instincts of self-preservation. Anything God asks you to do will have *life* in it. Any instinct that leads you to question God or avoid obedience to Him is misplaced and dangerous.

Paul the Apostle was at his most dangerous and effective place when he declared, "For to me, to live is Christ, and to die is gain."[10]

At Least I'll Die Moving Forward!

God is looking for people who have nothing to lose. He needs someone who understands what it is to say, "I'll die if I stay here in my crisis; I'll die if I try to go back into the mess I came from. So if I'm going to die, at least I'm going to die *moving forward*!"

It almost seems as if something inside those four hopeless lepers resonated with a silent message sent from heaven. Does God send signals of love, purpose, and direction to people who feel as if they are past hope? I think He does. His greatest signal, of course, was to send His only begotten Son.

The four forgotten lepers huddled against the wall of a city that had rejected them actually had a key role to play in God's divine drama that day. Everything hinged on their ability and willingness to risk what little they had for what they might gain.

God sends signals to us all the time. People who have "ears to hear" and "eyes to see" are sensitive enough in their spirits to hear those signals, but not everybody can perceive them. And many might refuse to act even if they understand the message.

In the physical realm, a wide variety of electromagnetic signals (radio signals) constantly pass through the atmosphere. It's happening now—right where you sit reading this book, radio and television signals are in the air. You can't see them, but if you have the proper receiver tuned in to the proper frequency, you can detect and decipher messages they are carrying.

If you have a cell phone and someone calls you, then you can pick up those signals. If you have the proper radio, then you can pick up and listen to any FM, AM, or satellite radio signal passing by.

Give Me Someone Who Doesn't Care About Their Reputation

God was sending out signals about Israel through His prophets, but certain key people just refused to listen. He was saying, "I want to set the nation free and liberate My people from the Syrian army. I just need somebody to move. That king has a '*heart*' problem, and his general has a '*hearing*' problem. They were both set in place to lead and protect—it seems they believe they have too much to lose. Is anyone listening down there?"

Whenever "important" or "leading" or "qualified" people refuse to listen or obey, then God gets to the point where He says, "I'll take anybody." The "anybody" He takes is often the person who has nothing to lose, who is not trying to preserve his or her reputation.

> "If they receive us we'll live, if they kill us we'll die. We've got nothing to lose."
>
> So after the sun went down they got up and went to the camp of Aram [Syria]. When they got to the edge of the camp, surprise! Not a man in the camp! The Master had made the army of Aram hear the sound of horses and a mighty army on the march. They told one another, "The king of Israel hired the kings of the Hittites and the kings of Egypt to attack us!" Panicked, they ran for their lives through the darkness, abandoning tents, horses, donkeys—the whole camp just as it was—running for dear life.[11]

This Is the Only Reasonable Answer: God Did It!

What happened? How could a battle-hardened army of men who grew up in a society of raiders and fighters be so easily fooled and spooked in the night? The only reasonable answer is given in Scripture: *God did it.*

We know three things about this moment in history:

1. The four lepers decided they had nothing to lose, and as the sun went down, they started marching from the gate of the city toward the Syrian camp on their bandaged and crippled feet.
2. The Syrian army thought they were hearing the sound of horses and a mighty army marching their way.
3. God was involved.

The Bible doesn't spell out the divine methods involved, but it sure gives us a strong hint that those lepers were involved in some way. Could it be that anytime you turn toward the promise and away from the past, angels fall in step behind you, marching with you to your destiny?

When They Started Marching, So Did God

Those lepers had decided that at the very least, a quick death is better than a slow one. It is interesting to me that *when they started marching, apparently, so did God.*

God was on the move! Often the only thing necessary to get God to move is for *man to move first!*

Since these men had lived with leprosy for some time, their bodies were undoubtedly showing the strain. The famine hadn't helped things either. They must have been emaciated, weak, and unsteady on their feet.

Even the act of clambering to their feet may have been a major challenge that left them breathless. After checking to rewrap their crippled feet, and carefully covering their disfigured faces in the twilight, they moved out. Pushing away from the stonework wall of the city, they began shuffling with uncertain rhythm toward the Syrian camp in the distance.

The farther they went, the more resolve they felt. Their feet began to move together as if to a unified beat, and perhaps they began to pick up the pace. They could actually smell the food simmering in the Syrian pots long before they could see anything.

We learned from the experience of Naaman the leper that God is waiting for an excuse to bless you. The obedience of the four lepers to their inner prompting linked with their risk-it-all attitude gave God the excuse He was looking for.

Your weakness is stronger than your enemy's strength when God amplifies it!

God could have used four nobles or five city elders, or a single king from Samaria, but He didn't. He could have hand-chosen four Israeli Green Berets or Samarian SEALs—but none of them seemed to be listening that night. The only ones willing to step up were four lepers. And that was all He needed to break the enemy's choke hold on the city.

The Bible tells us the four lepers started walking, and roughly during the same period the Syrians started hearing things . . . *big* things, *loud* things, sounds like warhorses and a mighty army of foot soldiers on the march.

Never Underestimate the Power of Four Limping Lepers

This is what I suspect happened: God amplified the eight feet of those four determined lepers as they marched. Their path perhaps was marked with bloodstained footprints.

When God turns up the amplifier, He can make eight shuffling feet sound like an army. The enemy hears you coming—even in your *weakness*—if you have a "nothing-to-lose" attitude! The Bible says, "When I am weak, then I am strong."[12] Your weakness is stronger than your enemy's strength when God amplifies it!

Is it possible that this "battle" outranks even the improbable adventures of Gideon and his army of three hundred lamp-breakers and horn-blowers?

Gideon's unlikely band of heroes managed to rout an army of 135,000.[13] Yet, here we have four limping lepers who "routed" a great army of Syrian besiegers without even a single weapon!

Can you hear God leaning over the ramparts of heaven and calling to His archangels, Michael and Gabriel:

> Hey, boys, take the microphone down there to the road leading out of Samaria. Put it real close to the ground and amplify the sound of those feet. You know the ones, the bloody footprints marching toward My purposes. That rhythmic shuffle pleases Me—it is the music of obedience to Me. Turn it up—more—more! Let the earth shake with the glory of My praise! Let My enemies be scattered with the sound of eight obedient feet moving to do My will.

The four lepers didn't have a clue about the power of fear being loosed on the enemy. Step after step they moved toward God's purposes. Soon they would witness its aftermath.

When they reached the far outskirts of the vast sea of tents at the Syrian camp, they might have hesitated, half convinced they would be arrow-shot on sight. They could smell the food cooking on hundreds of different cooking fires.

Perhaps the four chose the youngest and most mobile of the group to sneak up closer to the campfires and give a report. When he finally shuffled back to their hiding spot, he confirmed what their noses and growling bellies had already told them.

The Syrians had some meat cooking on the barbecue grill—it looked like they had lamb on the menu that night. Maybe big batches of lentils simmered over the campfires, and candles were lit to ward off the growing darkness of twilight. "I think everybody is eating right now—maybe they are all in their tents. No one was hanging around the campfires," the scout said.

All four of these lepers were hungry—they hadn't eaten anything in days, and they hadn't eaten *well* since their diagnosis long ago, much less the seven-year famine. Once the scout made his report, the other three lepers became even more restless.

> "If they kill me, they kill me. But I refuse to let those lamb ribs burn on that grill!"

How long could they stand to stay hidden on the outskirts of the camp, only a matter of a few yards from the feast of their lives? They were at the point of starvation, and finally, they just couldn't take it anymore.

One of the lepers tells the others: "You know, maybe they *are* sitting in their tents, and when we walk over there they just might shoot us in the back with arrows. Do we really care? At least we have a chance to get something to eat before we die."

Then one of the lepers in the back punches the bony torso of the youngest leper in front. "You go first."

"No, I'm afraid. No way."

Finally, the oldest and most grizzled one of the four stands up and says: "Well, you know what? I'm going to go in. If they kill me, they kill me. But I refuse to let those lamb ribs burn on that grill!"

You have to admit, there are some admirable characteristics about these four lepers. For one thing, those four men came to the point where they said, "Enough is enough!"

Start Marching Toward the Promise

Perhaps you have reached that point in life where you know you'll lose only if you stay *where* you are and *the way* you are. You have nothing to lose, so why not put your hope in God. Start marching toward the promise. Tell yourself and anyone else who is listening, "If I'm going to die, at least I'm going to die going the right way. Why sit here till we die?"

"What good is it going to do if I go look for a job?"

"What good will it do to attempt to start over at my age?"

"What good will it do to keep on trying? My spouse is gone and the children are out of control."

"What good is it going to do if I write that letter and try to heal that relationship? I already know what they're going to say. For years they've said they don't want to talk to me."

Take a lesson from some lepers who said, "Look, we are going to die *here*, or we are going to die *there*, so at least we should die moving in the right direction!"

There comes a time when you just have to make up your mind and *do something*. Draw a line in the sand! Make your stand! Declare out loud, "I am not going to run or turn away anymore. This time I am not going to back up." Remember—when you are down to nothing, God is up to something!

When Namaan obeyed the prophet of God and dipped himself seven times in the river Jordan, he was healed because he *obeyed* the word of God. There wasn't anything special about the muddy water. He wasn't healed by the water.

Beware the Thundering Sound of Obedience!

When the four lepers started walking on the road from Samaria, there wasn't anything special or magical about that road. And there was nothing unique about those lepers that frightened away the Syrian army—the enemy was frightened by the *thundering sound of their faith and obedience!* The enemy army retreated in fear as the lepers advanced in faith. The fight was finished before it started.

There was another time when One who many considered an unlikely hero also left a trail of bloody footprints. They led from a city to the place of God's highest purpose.

Those footprints of obedience stained the ground red with the sin of thousands of generations. But they shook the earth and ended in a twilight battle of the rejected against the rebellious. When that wounded Hero returned from the battlefield, He held captivity captive and carried with Him the keys to hell and death itself. He confiscated the keys from their previous possessor.[14]

That was when God drew a line in the sand and said, "It is finished," and hell screamed, "We have a Visitor!"

What happens when the Promise visits the curse? Hell evacuates on credit. Satan leaves! He can't even stay around for the final conflict . . . he already knows the outcome.

"If I'm Going to Die, I'm Going to Die Eating"

The old leper quickly shuffled out of his hidden place of safety and into the clearing between the forest and the campsite; then he headed for the largest rack of ribs he could see.

Glancing nervously from left to right, he grabbed the roasting ribs and circled back to hide behind a bush and began to gnaw, expecting any minute for an arrow to pierce his side or a spear to be thrust through him from the darkness. But he said, "If I'm going to die, I'm going to die eating."

When the other three watched him grab those mouthwatering ribs *without getting attacked*, they turned to one another simultaneously and said, "That other rack of ribs is mine!"

Their entire focus for the next five minutes was to be the first to latch onto a rack of ribs and wolf down as much as possible without breathing or stopping to chew. Then the reality of where they were suddenly dawned on them. When they sheepishly looked up and glanced around at their surroundings, they realized (thankfully) that there was no one in the nearby Syrian tent.

Perhaps, assuming that all of the former residents were called to some meeting in the middle part of the camp, the lepers cautiously peeked inside a second tent. (This part is in the Bible! You won't believe it if you don't read it.)

These four lepers entered the camp and went into a tent. First they ate and drank. Then they grabbed silver, gold, and clothing, and went off and hid it. They came back, entered another tent, and looted it, again hiding their plunder.[15]

The Bible says the lepers helped themselves to the free food and drinks, and then they helped themselves to the free silver, gold, and clothing. They began to go from tent to tent gathering the loot, taking a break only to hide everything from view. *A hoarding, hiding mentality is not the will of a sharing, caring God!*

> **A hoarding, hiding mentality is not the will of a sharing, caring God!**

Ask the Israelites in the wilderness about hoarding! They tried to hoard God's provision of food—the manna from heaven—only to find it infested with maggots once their illicit treasure was kept beyond God's prescribed "expiration date." The hoarded manna spoiled. How many people have maggots in their manna because of a hoarding mentality?

As soon as the lepers hid their plunder, something incredible happened that still sends shivers up my spine thousands of years later. One of them said, "We do not well . . ."[16]

Can you see these lepers wearing portions of splendid Syrian uniforms hastily thrown over the rags of cursed outcasts, with silver coins and jewelry still clutched in their hands?

> **We do not well . . .**

Now imagine what happened when one of them—perhaps the old grizzled one—suddenly said to his companions, "*Uh-oh, I've got a bad feeling about this. This isn't right!*" In biblical lingo the phrase is, "*We do not well.*"

There is a first step to "the ultimate turnaround," and it is simply *to turn around . . .*

CHAPTER 9

I've Got Good News and I've Got Bad News

First, the Bad News . . .

The bad news is you messed up. You failed the test, you lost your scholarship, you washed out, you must go to the back of the line. The good news is that you get to take the test again.

"We do not well."

This statement triggered an alarm in my mind and spirit as I searched the Bible for answers to the mystery of Gehazi's reappearance. What transformed this man from leprous outcast to royal insider? And when did it happen?

Step-by-step, I pored over the story of Gehazi's fall from favor. I read and reread the passages describing the time Gehazi and his sons received the curse of leprosy that had plagued Naaman the Syrian.

Then I began to systematically search specific Scripture passages for key words or word pairs that might give me some clue to unlock this mystery.

The more I read and meditated over the story of the four lepers, the more my imagination came alive under the inspiration of the Holy Spirit. I could almost see the scene play out before my eyes . . .

> The leper's gnarled right hand fumbled at another half-hidden
> sack of silver, as he struggled to carry a large bundle of beautiful
> garments draped across his scaly left arm. It was on his second

trip from the camp en route to stash his loot behind some thorny bushes when the thought penetrated his brain like a sharp arrow striking a target.

There was something "déjà vu-like" about this eerie scene. *I've been here before. There is something about all of this that makes me feel uneasy*, the grizzled old leper thought to himself. Trying to dismiss that feeling, perhaps he shrugged his shoulders as he pondered, *How else would you feel in an enemy encampment?*

Glancing down at his pile of salvaged riches, perhaps the old leper saw an insignia of the Syrian kingdom flash by his eyes as he dumped a handful of coins into the velvety Syrian garment he left there on the second trip. The shock of the memory knocked him to his knees, and then the pain of that sudden movement sent waves of torment through his tortured limbs and rippled through the rest of his body. He had seen just such an insignia before, on Naaman's silver!

Remembering the Last Illicit Touch

Adrenaline coursed through his system as he remembered the last time he had touched silver and garments from Syria. Naaman was a Syrian general!

Almost instantly, the leper threw the silver and garments to the ground, turned suddenly to face the three younger lepers and said, "We do not well."

"What do you mean, 'We do not well'? It looks to me like we're doing very well—and it is *about time!*"

"No, no, this isn't ours," the older man replied.

He couldn't shake the memory of the last time his hands illicitly touched silver and garments.

"We do not well."

Is it possible that the four lepers at the gate of Samaria included Gehazi? Was there some old memory that was triggered when that leper touched the Syrian silver and garments again? Could there be a connection here that could help explain Gehazi's restoration?

The Words of the Lepers Leaped Off the Page

I knew that Gehazi and his sons became lepers sometime *before* the beginning of the seven-year famine. *At the risk of being repetitious*, we have to ask in the light of this biblical conundrum, why Gehazi mysteriously reappeared in the king's palace in Samaria *at the exact end of the famine*—without the leprosy, and with no clue as to how it happened?

The words of the lepers leaped off the pages of God's Word:

> These four lepers entered the camp and went into a tent. First they ate and drank. Then they grabbed silver, gold, and clothing, and went off and hid it. They came back, entered another tent, and looted it, again hiding their plunder.
>
> Finally they said to one another, "*We shouldn't be doing this! This is a day of good news and we're making it into a private party! If we wait around until morning we'll get caught and punished.*"[1]

There is something odd about the story of the four lepers. It is easy to miss it at first, but upon close examination you may notice something that seems to imply some great failure or mistake in the past. "We'll get caught and punished." Who would catch them? Who would punish them?

As I read and reread this passage, I began to suspect a miracle in the works. We've already established the fact that Gehazi and his sons were hopeless lepers when Israel and Samaria plunged into the seven-year famine prophesied by Elisha.

We also know that Jewish law required lepers to remain outside the walls of major cities under most circumstances, keeping their distance from others to prevent cross infection and contamination. Segregation was the primary treatment for contamination, for it was written in the Law:

> And the leper in whom the plague is, his clothes shall
> be rent, and his head bare, and he shall put a covering
> upon his upper lip, and shall cry, Unclean, unclean.
> All the days wherein the plague shall be in him he
> shall be defiled; he is unclean: *he shall dwell alone; with-*
> *out the camp shall his habitation be.*[2]

A strong *added* link to Gehazi's life showed up in this passage—***the illicit hoarding of silver and precious garments***. If the case wasn't already strong enough to produce a link, then along came the lepers' sudden attack of conscience. No one can be sure, but the mounting evidence seemed to indicate to me that this was the missing piece to the puzzle of Gehazi.

I think there are too many common threads to be coincidental.

1. Location—Samaria
2. Outside the city
3. Sudden attack of conscience when touching Syrian silver and garments

I began to wonder if anyone else had pondered the same conclusion.

Intensive research among various Jewish rabbinical writings on this story produced something very significant.

In general, the rabbis of previous centuries haven't been kind to Gehazi. But I was not surprised to see these words surface from many rabbinic writings about Gehazi. One noted rabbinical scholar, Rabbi Johanan wrote:

> The four lepers at the gate announcing Sennacherib's
> defeat were Gehazi and his three sons.[3]

God really does do some of His best work in secret. Perhaps Gehazi's submersion in the no-man's-land of leprosy and anonymity marks the place of his hidden identity. Was this the hidden place where God was preparing one of His most remarkable—and one of the least known—miracles of restoration? Buried deep within the biblical account are hints at Gehazi's identity. I can't prove this . . . after all, God does His best work in secret.

Setup for a Second-Chance Miracle

I believe Gehazi underwent seven long years of tutorial preparation as a leper. If the rabbinic supposition is true, then perhaps Gehazi didn't realize he was about to get a second chance. On the evening he and his sons decided to risk everything for a meal in the Syrian camp, God set him up for a divine rerun. The mercy of a retest. You remember your school days? How fondly do you recall the teacher who would mercifully give the test again (and drop the lowest score!)?

Gehazi was about to face a midnight test of his character, with the lives of thousands resting in the balance. If he and his companions had hoarded the silver and refused to spread the news of the Syrian retreat, the people of Samaria would continue to die needlessly.

If what the rabbis said and what I think was true, then God was returning Gehazi to the very test he had failed seven years earlier. He was about to face the temptation to repeat the very sin that landed him in the hell of leprosy the first time.

Now, Gehazi, *who was condemned seven years earlier over the illicit acquisition of silver and garments,*[4] would have the opportunity to save himself and the city by passing the test and not touching the silver the second time. That is God's designated doorway to restoration. The only way out of your mess is to take the test again.

There's no magic time period. Gehazi's seven-year sentence was not dependent upon *time served;* it was dependent upon *character changed.*

Sometimes character change takes longer due to the stubbornness of the individual. It's a state of repentance and rehabilitation that the ultimate Teacher is trying to create.

Again, the good news is that you will get to take the test again. The bad news is that for some, it takes forty years. The children of Israel wandered through the wilderness for forty more years *after* they stood at the border of the Promised Land and gazed at their inheritance from the painful position of doubt and unbelief.

I don't know about you, but personally, I don't want to stand with my toes at the edge of my promise, only to have to wander through a desert for forty more years before I'm given the opportunity to possess that promise! I want to pass the test!

But . . . if I fail the test, and I do not get discouraged and quit school, I will get the opportunity to take the test again, and again, and again . . .

What I personally have learned from our Master Teacher is this, "If you do not quit, you cannot fail."

If you do not quit, you cannot fail.

God is not interested in the amount of time that you spend in self-imposed exile away from your promise. He doesn't care about the amount of time spent in the prison of pain or the lap of spiritual leprosy. He doesn't care about the time, He cares about the *test*. He wants to know if the wisdom is there for a comeback.

For the children of Israel, it took forty years for them to pass the test. At any point, God could have directed them on a quick detour that would have led them straight to the Promised Land.

Acknowledge to the Teacher that you need private tutoring. The shortest path between your failures and God's favor is humility. Remember that the Teacher is always silent during a test. Ask for instruction *before* the test. Ask Him to teach you, and at some point in life, you will be given the opportunity to take the same test.

The shortest path between your failures and God's favor is humility.

"Don't quit school, take the test again. Persevere, don't quit."

You can come back from a red "F" on a test paper. You can still pass! Embarrassment can sometimes cause teens to drop out of school because they dread graduating later than their peers. (If this describes you, think about it. By the time you are thirty, it won't make any difference whether you graduated at seventeen or eighteen years of age. All that matters is that you graduate!)

Never, ever, let your past dictate your future.

Never let embarrassment over your present situation cause you to drop out of the race. The Christian walk has always been about *finishing* well—and it takes God's help to do it. Lean on Him. Never, ever, let your past dictate your future.

Gehazi the forgotten leper found himself face-to-face with his past and was offered a divine opportunity to rewrite his destiny.

"This is not right."

"What do you mean this is not right? This sure smells right, this feels right! These are real ribs in my belly, and clothes for my back, and gold and silver for my future—however long *that* will be. This has got to be right."

And one of them—no one but God really knows which one of them—repeated what he said earlier: "This isn't right. We do not well."

Something in the back of his mind said, *The last time I did this is what got me in this mess. Nope, I am not going to fail that test again.*

"Put it back."

"What do you mean, 'Put it back'?"

"Put back the silver and the garments. This is not just *our* victory. There are a whole lot of people starving in that city. We cannot just sit here. This is for them too. Put it back."

"What do you mean, 'Put it back'?"

"I mean, put it back."

"What are we going to do?"

"We're going to go tell the king."

This time around, just as it was the first time, apparently no one was watching to pass judgment on his actions. The lepers were alone in the camp.

The first time silver and garments were connected with Gehazi, he carefully engineered his deception of Naaman and the prophet Elisha. Then he executed his plan with practiced precision and a calm confidence that he would not be caught. He was shocked to discover that the eyes of God are not limited by time, space, or carefully crafted subterfuge. Elisha's reputation as a seer proved to be true—he saw Gehazi's actions.

The "Put It Back" Principle

Anytime you "take" anything out of God's hands, He will let you have it. On the other hand, He will take care of anything that you put into His hand. There is a big difference between taking and receiving. If it is a gift from God, receive it with thanksgiving. If it is something reserved for the Lord, don't touch it, claim it, covet it, manipulate it, or gain glory from it. Put it back! Pass the test! God is watching!

Motivated by Survival and Desperation

In this second test, there was no preplanning or careful execution of a plot. Gehazi and his sons acted under the motivation of survival and desperation. Even though no one was looking, they still acted as if their theft was wrong. They hid their loot! From whom? They hid it from a guilty conscience as if it would be taken from them if discovered.

If this had taken place in the climate of our culture today, I'm sure many would rush to argue the side of the lepers, citing their poverty and the extreme prejudice they endured. We want to justify our "I needed it" mentality and defend our "I needed it more than them" attitude. The problem is that this was a test leading to a second chance and a new beginning—one that was unexpected and that most people would say was undeserved.

Gehazi probably didn't even know he was facing a test—just as you and I rarely perceive tests in our lives until later. One thing we should remember is that God is always interested in the heart, not in our high-sounding arguments or lengthy justifications.

Given the gift of failure seven years before, would this man, Gehazi, learn from his mistake and transform his failure into a new future? Would he successfully negotiate this test and enjoy a second chance?

Did you note what I said—"the *gift* of failure"? We often learn more from our failures than our successes.

Presumption Never Mixes Well with Destiny

Whether or not he understood the reasoning at the time he suddenly backed away from the illicit silver and garments, Gehazi still knew the hard-won principle of obedience: *Presumption never mixes well with destiny.*

We already know the outcome because we enjoy the benefit of hindsight. It is a matter of history for us. For Gehazi on that dark night when he endured the trial of his soul, nothing was certain except his sentence of lifelong leprosy and an inner conviction that he would *not* make the same mistake twice. Perhaps no one was looking, but it didn't matter. This time, he would do the right thing.

Failure is often the womb of success!

Failure can be our best teacher, but many people don't seem to realize it. For instance, one of the latest trends in some schools is to eliminate grades because of the possibility that failure may somehow permanently damage students.

History would say otherwise. I've studied and analyzed human events all my life; it is part of my general fascination with history. Even a quick survey of the historical record reveals the prevailing wisdom of thousands of generations and civilizations on the subject: failure is a master incentive for success. In fact, *failure is often the womb of success!*

Failure is not your enemy! Failure can be a faithful friend that speaks the truth to you. *Not to learn from failure*—now *that* kind of ignorance is an enemy to run from!

Finishing well is our ultimate goal, but failure is often the first foundation stone we receive to help us reach that goal. The only thing about failure that is permanently damaging is the misconception that we are doomed to remain there.

God's method shows up again and again in His Word. If you fail the test it doesn't frustrate God, He has all the time in the world. It may take a little extra time, but in due season He will bring you back to the same place so you can take that test again.

If you don't cross the Jordan, then be prepared to take another lap around the wilderness. (And God doesn't grade "on the curve." You advance only by passing your test.)

And the way you pass the test is to take a lesson from Gehazi. He *remembered his failure* in the first test. It is possible that your mind may be saying, "Isn't it a stretch to connect Gehazi to these four unnamed lepers?"

I Decided There Had to Be a Connection

All I can answer is that it was a stretch for me too until I discovered that *the mistake Gehazi made seven years earlier was exactly the same mistake these four lepers chose not to make the day before the famine ended miraculously*. At that point I decided there had to be a connection.

As I noted earlier, I discovered that many rabbinical scholars have pondered the same thing over thousands of years, and I found some of them that came to the same conclusion and wrote about it also.[5]

Again, God does His best work in secret. I don't *know* how it happened, but I am convinced that this *could be* how it happened. In any case, we do know it happened somehow: Gehazi came back.

How can you come back from a major failure or disappointment in life?

Be faithful. Keep moving toward the promises of God in your life.

Don't touch what He told you not to touch. Be obedient to pick up the things He tells you to pick up.

"Yeah, but I've already failed those tests."

Be prepared—you *will* be given the chance to take that test again.

There will come a point when you may realize you are going through the same processes or challenges that defeated you once before in your life. Be of good courage. God will give you the grace to pass the test that you failed the first time.

"You don't understand. I've relived that failure every night since it happened. No matter what I do, no matter what drug I take or who I am with, I can't shake the guilt and shame of my failure."

Jesus Purchased Your Freedom from Failure

Remember that God is on your side. Jesus loved you so much that He personally paid the price for your ultimate freedom from failure! God loves you, even in your failure, but He loves you too much to leave you there!

Trust God enough to let Him take you through situations similar to the circumstances where things went sour due to bad decisions, weakness, wrong motives, or difficult surroundings. When you pass the test, you give God the excuse to bless you and release Him to deliver you from the "leprosy" of failure and inadequacy.

You will no longer feel like an outcast. As far as your family, friends, and enemies are concerned, they will say, "One day you were down and out, and the next thing we knew you were restored and on the top of the world, whispering counsel in the king's ear."

Do you know anyone who is ready to experience some incredible restoration like that? If He can do it for Gehazi, He can do it for any-body—*including you.*

Remember that you are never more dangerous than when you have nothing to lose—even if your name is Gehazi.

Sometimes our supposed *success* leads us *back* to retake a test we passed earlier in life. In this case, success can become our worst enemy. There is nothing more dangerous than a man who has never experienced failure. The arrogance of success is an intoxicating drink, and it dulls the senses.

It can actually be more difficult to pass the test of success than the test of failure. We don't seem to learn as much from our successes as we do from our failures. This happened to Peter, whose *devastating personal failure* was predicted by Jesus, documented in the Bible, and highlighted in countless sermons over the ages.

Jesus warned proud Peter (who was glowing in the light of a success at the time) that Satan wanted to "sift" or test him. The Master Teacher actually announced a test; something He rarely does! Peter's response was to crow some on his own about how he would *never* deny Jesus, and how he would rather die with Him than deny Him. Jesus then prophesied that Peter would *deny* Him three times in a row before the roosters would crow, signaling the next sunrise.[6]

Sure enough, Peter denied even knowing Jesus in the court of Pilate—and even added some curse words for good effect. Peter failed. His bitterness only grew with the conviction that since Jesus had died, he would never have a chance to right his wrongs.[7] He was a good man who felt doomed to live the rest of his life because of his bad choices. He bore the bitterness or "leprosy" of his betrayal and denial of Jesus.

Peter, I Have Good News and I Have Bad News . . .

Jesus had other plans in mind. The *third time* Jesus revealed Himself to His disciples after His resurrection from the grave, He looked Peter in the eyes and asked *three times* if he loved Him—one time for each of Peter's public denials of Christ. In essence, Jesus was saying, "Peter, I have good news and I have some bad news."[8]

The good news was that he had a second chance—the bad news was that he would have the opportunity to keep the second part of his boast—Peter would one day lay down his life for his Lord.[9]

If Peter could fail *three times* before he passed, and then rise to prominence—*then so can you!*

So you haven't heard from that son in more than twelve years . . .

and you don't know what the doctor's diagnosis and prognosis may reveal this week. You're honestly afraid you have "ruined" your kids with your temper or workaholic ways. You've beaten yourself over your failures for years . . .

Understand this great foundation of restoration: Even if it *was* your fault, Jesus Christ is still your Savior.

The key to your future is learning, "I'm not going to touch what I shouldn't. I am going to make a change!" All it takes is obedience, not disobedience. We must all *change directions* if we expect to get different results when God brings us face-to-face with past failures.

So perhaps the important question at this point isn't "Where to from here?" but, "How do you get from *here* to *there?*"

Do you remember the "good news, bad news" phrase? Well, the bad news is that *sometimes you just have to go back.* If you missed the turn, then you must go around the block again. The good news is that once you do, you get to take the test again.

CHAPTER 10

I'm Going Back
Facing the Risk of Rejection

> Then [the lepers in the abandoned Syrian camp] said to
> one another, "We are not doing right. This day is a day of
> good news, and we remain silent. If we wait until morning
> light, some punishment will come upon us. *Now therefore,*
> *come, let us go and tell the king's household."*[1]

T his brief exchange of words conceals a major victory over at least
seven years of physical and emotional pain that the four lepers had
to overcome *before* they could take their first steps back toward their city.

Once they learned there was a way back, they still had to *go back*
and face the possibility of rejection.

It is likely that each of these men harbored up to *seven years* of
painful memories in their minds. They had vivid, full-color, wide-
screen, high definition panoramic visions of the steady stream of
daily insults, put-downs, snubs, sneers, cursing, and cruel jokes they
endured as lowly lepers and beggars.

Leprosy was more than a dreaded disease that afflicted innocent
victims unfortunate enough to acquire it. It was also viewed as God's
punishment for sins of presumption against His holy name.[2]

In Gehazi's case, we *know* this was the case. Elisha decreed that the
leprosy of Naaman would come upon Gehazi and his descendants
forever because of his greed, his disobedience to God, and his
attempt to deceive God's servant.[3]

By the skewed standards of modern society, Gehazi and his leprous sons would have every right to hate the residents of Samaria. Those sons would have even *more* reason to *hate their father*! After all, what part did they play when their father committed the sin that condemned him *and them* to the banished life of lepers, walking dead men living in endless torment and regret over what could have been if . . .

If this incredible true story were offered to Hollywood producers, they would be sorely tempted to "revise and improve" the story to better follow politically correct form.

We could expect to see a new scene inserted featuring all four men arrayed in the finest Syrian robes on a hill overlooking the city of their torment. As they dine on the best of food, we could expect to hear choice comments of bitter revenge and cynical laughter spliced between scenes of personal suffering and savagery inside the city walls.

The movie might end with dramatic final scenes of the city being consumed by fire. "They rejected us when we needed them. No way am I going to help them now."

Gehazi and his sons passed the primary test when they laid down their illicit silver, gold, and garments. They also passed a second test when they decided to return to the very city that had rejected them to share their good news and good fortune.[4]

How Were the Four Lepers Healed?

As I examined the Scriptures, I really began to wonder how Gehazi was healed. No one but God really knows how Gehazi and possibly his sons were healed of that incurable disease—especially when it was pronounced over them by one of the greatest of the Old Testament prophets.

These are the facts: Gehazi was a leper until he suddenly showed up again in the king's court *immediately after the famine ended*. That event happened approximately seven years to the day after the prophet warned the Shunammite woman about the famine. The same woman and her son walked in on cue just as Gehazi was finishing what appears to be his *first* story about Elisha at the request of the king (so he hadn't been there very long).

One Stood Out from All the Rest

After searching the Scriptures again for any incidents involving lepers being healed, I found several miraculous healings described, but one stood out from all the rest. It involved a New Testament story about Samaritan lepers who had a miraculous encounter with Jesus. In Samaria, again! (Note that they "stood afar off," honoring the segregating edict.)

> Now it happened as [Jesus] went to Jerusalem that He passed through the midst of *Samaria* and Galilee.
>
> Then as He entered a certain village, there met Him ten men who were lepers, who stood afar off.
>
> And they lifted up their voices and said, "Jesus, Master, have mercy on us!"
>
> So when He saw them, He said to them, "Go, show yourselves to the priests." And so it was that *as they went*, they were cleansed.[5]

The lepers who were healed by Jesus in Samaria were cleansed *as they went*. Could it be that the process of *obedience*, which may include dipping, worshipping or walking, is the process of cleansing and healing?

If this is true, then could it set up a simple biblical principle? One that may be extended and extrapolated to the Old Testament account of these four lepers—and to Gehazi in particular? In both situations, we find lepers who were mysteriously transformed from hopeless victims of aggressive leprosy to totally cleansed men in one day! (And in Samaria, no less!)

Healed as They Went . . .

The Bible says the lepers in the New Testament were cleansed and healed *"as they went."* Could it be that *after* Gehazi and his sons laid down their illicitly acquired silver and garments and decided to return to the city to tell the king . . . that they were healed *"as they went"* back down the road leading to Samaria? Is it possible that the miracle of deliverance occurred as they marched toward the camp in obedience, and the miracle of healing came when they marched away from the camp toward the city?

No one really knows, but somewhere along the road it must have happened or at least begun. Was it on the first step, the fifth step, or after the first mile? We don't know how or when, but we know that it happened somewhere, somehow.

Was Naaman healed on his first dip, on his second dip, or on the seventh? Was it progressive or sudden? Did he have seven scabs on his face and every time he went down one came off? We don't know.

All we know about Gehazi is that he was a leper, and somehow, by the time he showed up in the king's court, he was *healed*.

When I think about that long night and day, it is easy to be overwhelmed by what may have actually happened.

The Bloody Footprints Grew Fainter

Who noticed that when they began their journey back toward the city, the four lepers left bloody smudges on the road where they walked with their bandaged feet? With each step the men made toward the purposes of God, the bloody footprints grew fainter and fainter until they disappeared altogether.

The men probably didn't notice—but perhaps their toes had begun to grow back as they drew nearer the city gate.

Perhaps their faces were carefully veiled in accordance with Levitical law, and in the darkness of the early morning hours, they couldn't have noticed that their facial features were changing—for the better.

The white scaly patches were falling off while noses and ears were growing back. Could it be possible that by the time the men reached the city gate, the skin on their bodies had already been made as fresh and new as baby's skin? It happened for Naaman and the ten lepers, why not Gehazi and the other three lepers?

It is the same with us. Many times, you will not realize until later that God's restoration in your life has already been working! Sometimes we fail to recognize God's miracle in our lives until someone else points out the obvious.

The Bible record reveals to us these details about what else happened that night:

> Then they said to one another, "We are not doing right. *This day is a day of good news, and we remain silent.* If we wait until morning light, some punishment will come upon us. *Now therefore, come, let us go and tell the king's household.*"
>
> So they went and called to the gatekeepers of the city, and told them, saying, "We went to the Syrian camp, and surprisingly no one was there, not a human sound— only horses and donkeys tied, and the tents intact."
>
> And the gatekeepers called out, and they told it to the king's household inside.[6]

How Could You Forget? We Are Lepers!

When Gehazi realized that the miraculous flight of the Syrians wasn't just about them, he said, "We have to tell others, we must tell the king." I can almost see his sons jerk back in surprise, fully covered in the rags and bandages that marked hopeless lepers. I can hear them say, "Dad, even if we go, they won't let us enter the city. How could you forget? *We are lepers!*"

"I don't know about all of that, but I do know we *have to go*. If they won't let us in, then we'll stand outside the gates and shout our message until *somebody* hears us!"

When God restores you, He often has *more* in mind than you, your life, your family, your job, or even your present situation. The smallest details of your life do matter to Him, but God does things on a cosmic scale. He may have something bigger in mind, even when He appears to be working small miracles in our lives.

Perhaps I should say it this way: When God used the four lepers to bring deliverance, I imagine He was saying, "I've been *looking for some-*

body. I want to set the whole city free. These four will do just fine—there is no way they will take the credit, or touch the glory."

Take heart! You will do just fine for God's use.

God restores you so that you can bring restoration to others. He always uses *people* like you and me to *do* things, *cause* things, *create* things, *restore* things, and *ignite change*.

Even after Gehazi and his sons passed the test of the illicit silver and garments, and then passed the second test by choosing to return to the city where they had been outcasts for seven years, they would now face yet another indignity on the path of obedience.

Sometimes the very people who need the good news you have, choose to isolate themselves from you.

Don't Shoot the Messenger Before Hearing the Message

People may sever you from their lives because of your past, remembering your history and all the things that didn't go well in your life. You may remind them of a painful memory or of their own weaknesses or failures. Even though you have what they need, some people want to shoot the messenger before hearing the message!

It happened often in the New Testament. We know how Jesus, the perfect Messenger with the perfect Message, was rejected and crucified without cause.

Even the woman at the well of Samaria probably felt there was no doubt she would be rejected by her townspeople because of her ruined reputation, even though she was bringing the greatest news her village could ever hear.

She confessed to Jesus that she had been through five marriages, and she was living with a man who wasn't her husband. Those aren't exactly the credentials of an anointed evangelist. The woman knew it was very unlikely that anyone in her village would listen to her, but she went back there anyway.

Can you see the faces of the villagers, their eyes rolling, when the five-time divorcee says, "Come meet a Man!" *Yeah, and how many men have we already met? This is just another to share your bed.*

Thank God she refused to give up. "I've got to tell you about this Man! I have good news to tell you. Somebody, anybody, will you just check out my story? It sounds too good to be true, but come meet a Man who told me everything about my past. He said He is the Promised One. Come with me, and meet Him for yourself!"

After one encounter with Jesus at the well, this woman with a ruined reputation became the ideal messenger with the most effective testimony for reaching that village! One translation of this Bible passage says, "The people came *streaming* from the village to see him"![7] Our *history* of failure can become "His-story" of grace!

Can We Really Afford to Remain Silent?

God will use you to bring freedom to more than just you or your family. But first He will use your restoration as a launching point to restore others.

> We are not doing right.
> This day is a day of *good news*,
> and *we remain silent*.[8]

Faced with this honest statement of the four lepers, how many people would be "weighed in the balance and found wanting"?

How many "hoard" the good news of the gospel and rarely lead people to the eternal hope of Jesus Christ?

When we all stand before God, who will volunteer to take the impossible task of explaining why we remained silent when we had good news that could save our cities and transform our nation?

Restoration is worth facing the risk of rejection.

As the four lepers walked back toward the city, they were probably thinking about the reception they would receive at the city gate.

What do *you* do when you've messed up? When you've been rehired after being fired, how do you feel on your first day back at work? Perhaps this helps us understand in some small way how these lepers felt as they approached the wall and city gate that had become the boundaries of their public prison over the last seven years. "Who in the king's palace would believe a leper?"

Your mind may be locked into an arena dominated by past mistakes or circumstances also.

"Who will hire someone with a record?"

"Who would marry me? I've been divorced."

"Who would trust me after what I've done?"

Yes, you may encounter some difficulties. People may not trust you initially or even want to hear what you have to say. But . . . *the potential for restoration is worth facing the risk of rejection.*

The possibility of you receiving a new future in Christ may seem impossible to those around you. Your second chance and new beginning may be so unbelievable that even the best among all of your family and friends may have a hard time with your news.

I've gathered, from my study of the Bible, that the king of Israel had such a hard time accepting the leper's news that he announced publicly to his staff that it was a trap.

So don't be surprised if you hear people say, "We've seen this before. We've heard you make promises, and we've seen what usually happens later. You always fall back, you do the drugs again, you drink again, you betray our trust; you are hopeless. You just can't conquer your past."

Some Doubt There Is Anything to Gain; You Have Nothing to Lose!

The king doubted there was anything to gain, but Gehazi and his sons had nothing to lose. So they marched up to the scarred city gate in the predawn darkness and started shouting.

"Hey, h-e-l-l-o there! Yoo-hoo!"

Finally, a grouchy (*and* probably hungry) guard with a flickering torch peers down at the four men in the dim light and growls, "What do you old lepers want?"

"Yeah, I know we're just old lepers. That's okay, but we just need to tell you something. We went to the enemy's camp, and . . . he's *gone!*"

"You are delirious. You don't know what you're talking . . ."

"No, I'm telling you! There is food that is ready to eat around abandoned campfires! There's more than enough for the whole city! And it's getting cold right now; you need to go tell the king. Hurry!"

Thinking the Worst, Expecting the Worst, Planning for the Worst

Once the news sputtered its way up the royal chain of command and reached the king, the true state of his thinking quickly broke through his thin facade of royal stability. In his rebellious state, he was anything but stable or faithful. He was thinking the worst, expecting the worst, and planning for the worst.

God must have been the farthest thing from this king's mind, because he was living in a world of despair, hopelessness, and outright unbelief.

> So the king arose in the night and said to his servants, "Let me tell you what the Syrians have done to us. They know that we are hungry; therefore they have gone out of the camp to hide themselves in the field, saying, 'When they come out of the city, we shall catch them alive, and get into the city.'"[9]

True or Too Good to Be True?

The king was so bitter and cynical that he was convinced there was foul play involved! He said, "It's a trick! Yep, it's a trick. Those sneaky Syrians have abandoned camp all right, but they're pulling one of the oldest tricks in the book. They want us to come outside the city walls so they can capture us *alive!*" Sometimes good news is *so good* that everybody believes it is just *too good* to be true.

The king insisted, "It can't be," but when his servants begged him to check it out, he finally agreed. They must have had some difficulty finding chariot drivers desperate, delirious, or unfortunate enough to get chosen for the job. The king made it clear he believed it was a suicide mission.

The level of faith in the truth of this rumor matched the level of food remaining in the city—*none.* (When you're eating "donkey's head soup," you can't help but be stubborn!)

If you allow it, your enemy would like to see you wallow in the pool of self-pity, growing more helpless by the day as you say to yourself over and over again, "Nobody has had it as bad as me." *Your diet of doubt can hinder your restoration.* Feed your faith, not your fears!

What about you? Are you living in the shadow of your broken dreams, wondering what you did to deserve such pain and disappointment?

There Is a Path Out of Hell

Let me encourage you: Regardless of how bad you think your circumstances may be, *there is a path out of hell*—there is no limit to God's power to restore you. It begins with repentance, and the willingness to return to the point of your past failure and retake the test. Once you pass that test, you may find yourself walking and talking a new way.

> Okay, I've made my mind up. I know what *to* touch and what *not to* touch. I know where *to* go and where *not to go.* I know what *to* do, what *not to* do, I've learned from my mistakes. Now how do I get from here to there? ***I'm going back!***

Don't be surprised if God sends you *back* to bring good news, hope, and deliverance to others just like you! He did it with Gehazi and his sons.

What would have happened had the four lepers listened to logic or heeded their painful memories and just enjoyed their own private meal and personal treasure trove?

If the rabbinic interpretation is correct, and those four lepers at the gate were Gehazi and his sons, then I'm convinced they would not have been healed had they chosen *not* to pass the test of the silver and garments.

Their city and nation would have fallen into destruction and ultimate captivity sooner rather than later. The Syrian army would have caught on soon enough to return and reclaim everything the lepers tried to take in secret.

The four lepers answered the question "Where to from here?" Once they learned the way back, they chose to *go back* and face the risk of rejection. They marched back to their city to share their good news from God, and I believe they were healed as they went.

Again, let me tell you as plainly as I can—I'm talking about something *I do not know*. I don't know how Gehazi was restored. But I believe he was. This is the ultimate proof that God does His best work in secret.

I do not know how Gehazi got healed. I just know he did. We've provided every hint, scriptural clue, and rabbinical opinion we can lay our hands on; but again, in the final analysis—I'm talking about something *I do not know*. All I know is his final destination. He wound up in the king's court, and . . .

What happens next is almost beyond belief!

CHAPTER 11

Run Over By Good News!

Somebody's Coming Back—Make Sure It's You!

S tep back in our story about twenty-four hours. Three things were
happening roughly simultaneously. Gehazi's former boss, Elisha
the prophet, was having an interesting encounter with the rebellious
king of Israel.

First, King Jehoram was so angry over the chaos and desperation
in the capital city that he lashed out at Elisha the prophet and laid all
of the blame for the famine fiasco on him.

He vowed to have Elisha beheaded before the sun went down,
and sent a "messenger" or assassin to do the deed. The problem
that kings had with Old Testament prophets was that the prophets
had a habit of seeing and hearing the things their enemies plotted.
Forewarned is forearmed! Elisha gave instructions on how to deal
with the messenger and then proceeded to reel off a prophetic
announcement.

On that day, rebellion-induced famine and desperation had
reduced Samaritan society to eating its own children, and the prophet
that kings loved to hate said:

> Hear this message from the LORD! This is what the
> LORD says: *By this time tomorrow* in the markets of
> Samaria, five quarts of fine flour will cost only half

an ounce of silver, and ten quarts of barley grain will cost only half an ounce of silver.[1]

Then an official on whose hand the king leaned answered the man of God, and said, Behold, *if the* LORD *would make windows in heaven, might this thing be?* And (Elisha) said, Behold, *thou shalt see it with thine eyes, but shalt not eat thereof.*[2]

The prophet was predicting an overnight end to a seven year problem. The king was infuriated by this teasing prophetic announcement—but he was also shocked to discover that the powerful prophet Elisha already knew about the assassination plot and didn't even care!

Second, at the same time, a nameless leper with a deformed face and scarred body leaned against the wall of his besieged hometown, his thoughts consumed with hunger. He and his boys were still lost in the shadows of the forgotten, living under the hopeless curse of leprosy, and he sensed time was running out.

A Mother and Son Were Going to See the King

Third, many miles away, the Shunammite woman and her son packed for their trip to the capital city of Samaria, believing by faith that the old prophet Elisha had heard from God seven years earlier. She headed for a promise that had not yet come true.

The woman and her son returned from a far country at the appointed time to reclaim their land and possessions, and as often happens when pursuing a promise, they ran into present-day reality that apparently differed from the prophetic promise they had received.

Their house and lands were occupied, and *others* were reaping harvests from land and resources that actually belonged to the woman and her son. To this woman, the solution was simple. Go see the king. Their old friends who still lived in their old neighborhood probably told them they were crazy.

You just got back from out of town, so maybe you haven't been watching the local news. Don't you realize the king isn't gonna see you or anyone else?

Ben-hadad, the king of Syria, came back with his army! It was bigger than ever, and they surrounded the city and the king's palace. All hope is gone, and Syria has us locked in hopeless siege. CNN says people are actually eating donkey's heads and boiling their own kids in the city! And the place is just infested with lepers.

How could things ever get back to normal after a crisis like that? You had better stay away from there. If it was us, we'd forget about getting our house and land back.

We know you used to network with that old prophet, but don't put too much stock in what he said way back then. That was seven years ago. We all think he missed that prophecy. Things have changed since then. We are in an economic tailspin.

Unprepared for the Prophet's Sudden Response

The man "on whose hand the king leaned,"[3] a hand-picked royal official and personal assistant to Samaria's monarch, perfectly reflected his master's cynical view of life. Perhaps that is why they got along so well. This official *knew* the king hated it when the irritating old prophet started dispensing his unwelcome declarations—even this rare positive version.

This old prophet must have been in the sun too long during the famine! he thought, making no effort to conceal his well-timed smirk. He couldn't help but straighten out the old fool with some common sense when *Elisha* said, "*By this time tomorrow* . . . five quarts of fine flour will cost only half an ounce of silver . . . ten quarts of barley grain [for] only half an ounce of silver."

But no one—including the king's assistant—was prepared for the prophet's sudden response.

"You will see it, but not eat it!" The king's official sneered and did his best to laugh off the old seer's threat—first of all, who could believe such a stupid prediction about cheap flour and grain in abundance after a *seven-year drought?* And second, *if* such an outrageous thing should happen for some unknown reason, it was insane to assume *the man closest to the king* would see but *not* be allowed to eat any of it!

We see the same reaction today among people who mock ministers who talk about reward and punishment.

That court official actually had a lot of evidence weighing in on his side. Even logic and historic trends supported his statement of unbelief and cynicism over the upbeat prediction by Elisha. It wouldn't have been so bad if he hadn't tried to lump the "windows of heaven" into the equation. They weren't his or the king's windows—he couldn't open or close them. But God could.

He should have known better—the Bible doesn't tell us outright, but the man was probably Jewish. That means he probably grew up with the stories of God embarrassing the pharaoh of Egypt and dividing the Red Sea.

This was the God who opened barren wombs and provided manna out of heaven. Only a short period before that day (seven years or less), they had seen the prophet of God lead the entire army of King Ben-hadad himself to Samaria as if they were a nation of blind men! He should have known better, but he chose presumption over wisdom.

The King Had Already Put on His Grave Clothes

Restoration *was* highly unlikely for Samaria. The city was surrounded by a powerful, well-equipped army and led by a ruthless conqueror. The king had an apparent total of five horses left in his "royal stable" and no food for his few able-bodied soldiers (other than the horses).[4]

The city had been reduced to cannibalism, and the king already wore his grave clothes. We have to admit the improbability of Samaria's restoration.

Perhaps you sense the improbability of your restoration too. When the Word of the Lord finally comes to you, it will cause some people to say, "You couldn't be restored if God opened a window in heaven!" Just tell them stranger things have happened before!

The last words the king's arrogant assistant heard from the prophet that day were, *"You will see it happen, but you won't be able to eat any of it!"*[5] Then the old prophet dismissed him as if he wasn't worth the time of day and continued his meeting with the elders of Israel— excluding, of course, the king.

The long night began and the king grew more agitated by the minute. Perhaps he had just nodded off while still dressed in his sackcloth mourning clothes when his servants reluctantly woke him. What *more* could go wrong now?

When told of the rumor from the gatekeeper that the Syrians had fled their camp—*for no reason at* all—every paranoid bone in his body told him it was just another trap! Then he told his staff, "Let me now tell you what the Syrians have done to us. They know that we are hungry; therefore they have gone out of the camp to hide themselves in the field, saying, 'When they come out of the city, we shall catch them alive, and get into the city.'"[6]

Even though he just *knew* the Syrian king was up to something, he finally agreed to send someone to check out the ridiculous rumor about their army abandoning camp.

The sun was up by the time his charioteers returned with the unbelievable news.

It was true! The enemy was gone and there was food aplenty available in their encampment.

The lepers who discovered the victory were apparently forgotten during the miraculous melee that followed . . .

The Cynic Was Conspicuously Nervous All Night

The cynic, the man "on whose hand the king leaned," should have been nervous that morning. After he confirmed the news of the enemy's retreat and sudden abundance of food, perhaps he sighed and appeared to cheer up. *The old prophet was "half-right," then—even prophets miss it sometimes,* he thought to himself. *I guess I will be around to partake in the upcoming feast.*

As the king heard the news, perhaps he changed his clothes and threw his sackcloth outfit in the trash while calling for his top public official, the man "on whose hand the king leaned."

"If all of this is true, then when the announcement is made, people will stampede to get to the food and the city gate will fall into chaos. I will need my best man there—I want you to go down to oversee the opening of the gate. Make the announcement about the news and officially open the gate—*in my name, of course.* Make sure no Syrian plot is involved, and keep the crowd in line."

As the man turned to obey, perhaps the king added, "Report to me what you see and we'll have a celebratory breakfast together later. Maybe we'll enjoy some of this Syrian food they're talking about."

The rumor mill outpaced the king's official, and people heard about the food and the riches piled up in the abandoned Syrian campsite. The city gate was wide enough to accommodate a steady stream of carts, work animals, and pedestrians coming in and going out. But it was *never* designed to handle a wall of thousands of running, jostling, desperately hungry people who hadn't eaten for weeks.

The Bible tells us that in the mad rush through the gates, "the man upon whom the king leaned was trampled in the gates," fulfilling Elisha's prophecy to the letter. *Sometimes those who don't believe God's promises can get run over by good news!*

Do you remember the day when, like Job, *bad news* had to wait in line to get to you? There will come a day when *good news* will overwhelm your enemies! Your critics and adversaries will be run over by good news!

By the next day, the capital city of Samaria was eating well and the economy was bouncing back from the drought and the siege. God had supplied their need.

Have you noticed there is often something like "the aftermath of a miracle" in life? Remember: "It ain't over till it's over." Just like the days when bad news stacked up in your in-box—good news is *still* coming in.

Please Explain the "Syrian Thing"

Perhaps the king was standing beside his throne the next day, wondering who would ever replace his "right-hand" man. No likely candidates came to mind so he moved on to another topic that was bothering him. Turning to one of his orderlies, he summoned the chief night watchman from the main gate of the city. He launched an official investigation as to how all this good news came to be known.

"Now how did all this happen?" the king asked.

"How did what happen, Your Highness?"

"The Syrian thing."

"O-h-h, well, sir, you know we were guarding the city like *always*. And then those guys came, and they yelled at us in the middle of the night. So we woke up the prime minister, and the prime minister checked it out. Then he went in to wake you up. Anyway, you said, 'Be careful, it's probably a trap.'"

"*Who* told you?" the king asked. "You said, '*Those guys* . . .' What guys?"

"Well, sir, it was those three, no, there were four lepers, you know the ones who always hang out by the gate. They are just beggars cursed with leprosy. They are the ones who came that night and told us the enemy was gone."

"Lepers or not, I want to talk to them. Find them for me. Now!"

The king's royal command launched an all-out search for the four lepers who had saved the city. Could it be that the king's search team ran into a special problem that no one really anticipated?

Has Anyone Seen Four Ex-Lepers?

What if the search team discovered that no matter where they went, they could find no one who had seen four lepers in the city? Lepers were banned from the city, and all of the people they talked to, who actually stampeded through the city gate after the Syrian retreat, said they had other things on their minds.

The healing of leprosy couldn't have been a common thing. And how would you find four "ex-lepers" anyway? Even so, most Jews would remember the law that commanded anyone who felt they had been healed of leprosy to report to a priest for confirmation of their healing.

It may be a stretch, but what if one of the investigators located an old priest. What would a Levite or a priest think if four men showed up dressed as lepers, seeking certification of their miraculous cure under the old laws?

Biblically, if the men fully qualified as being cured under the Law, the priest could have certified them as whole after a time of quarantine, and sent them on their way in eight to fifteen days. (The only catch is that these men would stick out from the general population for a period of time—they were to shave off all their hair, including their eyebrows and beards.[7]) Perhaps it was just such a priest who steered the searchers in the right direction.

Think about the moment Gehazi and his sons *first realized* a miracle had taken place in their bodies. What kind of questions would they have asked one another? Those men must have asked some of the same questions you and I ask in our day.

If they were healed, "as they went," just as the lepers in Jesus's day were healed, then the moment when they realized "the change" had occurred to their crippled bodies must have made for some interesting drama. Let me speculate.

Gehazi, as the father and eldest member of the troop, may have been carrying a torch or lantern taken from the Syrian encampment. It was night. Their sole focus was the gate of Samaria, and each one of them must have wrestled with the foolhardy appearance of their decision to tell the king of their discovery.

When the tall gate loomed before them in the predawn darkness, all four of the men began to shout and yell.

"Hey, h-e-l-l-o there! Yoo-hoo! Wake up—we have good news!"

Remember the grouchy gatekeeper who finally showed up with the stub of a flickering torch; he just barely recognized the distinctive clothing identifying the four men as lepers. "What do you old lepers want?"

Gehazi winced at the insult, thinking, *You would think I'd be used to it by now.* Then he announced his good news of the Syrians' retreat to the skeptical gatekeeper. Meanwhile, his sons were making so much noise behind him that he could barely concentrate on his message.

"Hey, What Happened to Your Nose?"

What he didn't realize was that when the gatekeeper's sputtering torch illuminated the lepers from a fresh angle, one of Gehazi's sons released a startled gasp. Leaning forward, he jerked back the cloak that covered his brother's head and face.

"Hey, what happened to your nose?"

Irritated with the interruption, the brother pulled his cloak back into position and leaned forward to listen more closely to his father's dialogue with the doubtful doorkeeper.

Absentmindedly, he asked, "What do you mean, 'what happened to my nose?' You know I haven't had a nose in a long time. You don't have one either. Leprosy ate your nose away too."

"No, no. Listen, you've *got* a nose, and it's even better than that. The scar is gone, and so are the scars on your face. It's *all* gone."

"Have you been drinking too much of that Syrian wine? Nobody just grows back a nose! Now stop fooling around. It's not going so well with this grouch of a gatekeeper."

"Look, I'm not fooling around. I don't know *how* it happened, I don't know *when* it happened, and I definitely don't know *why* it happened. All I do know is that it *did* happen!"

"What . . . ?"

"You've got a nose!"

As the shocked brother excitedly felt the unfamiliar contours of his new face, the exchange between Gehazi and the gatekeeper became even more animated.

"You are delirious," the gatekeeper scoffed. "You don't know what you're talking . . ."

"No, I'm telling you! The Syrians are gone! And there is food ready to eat around their abandoned campfires! There's more than enough for the whole city! And it's getting cold right now; you need to go tell the king. Hurry!"

Dancing, Jumping, and Shouting Like Mad Men!

When Gehazi turned around, fighting his feelings of frustration and rising irritation over the confrontation with Old Grouchy, he couldn't believe his eyes. All three of his sons had thrown off their cloaks and kicked off the thick bandages that normally concealed their feet and hands. They were actually dancing, jumping, and shouting like mad men!

"It's gone! The leprosy is gone! Dad, look at our faces! Here, look at our feet! Count 'em—all *ten* toes. And look at our noses . . ."

Instantly, Gehazi's trembling hands flew to his face to confirm the impossible. His facial disfiguration—worse than any of his sons'—was completely gone. None of them noticed the grouchy doorkeeper. Just before he shuffled off to the king's palace, he'd lingered a moment with a puzzled look on his face, watching the antics of the four crazy lepers.

Who knows, but perhaps somewhere in the excitement over the news, the gatekeeper or his assistants left the gate totally unattended in their rush to notify the king's servants. Somehow, some way, the lepers slipped through the gate and vanished into the morning, leaving their distinctive outer garments in a pile just outside the city gate. No one knows for sure, but perhaps we may speculate that those lepers were on a mission of *obedience*—perhaps they had set a course to present themselves to the priest to certify their impossible cure!

Within the hour, the wheels of the king's chariots passed over the pile of clothes left by the former lepers, en route to investigate the outlandish claim that the Syrians had abandoned their camp and fled back across the river Jordan.

Finding the One upon Whose Arm the King Used to Lean

That same day in the aftermath of the stampede, the grouchy old gatekeeper found the mangled remains of the one upon whose arm the king *used* to lean, literally, the king's "right-hand" man.

While investigating the death of his court confidant and the incredible victory, questions begged answers. The king summoned his court assistants and interrogated the gatekeeper about the lepers. Then his search parties scoured the city until they finally found the four former lepers rejoicing in their homes with the families they hadn't seen for seven years.

This much we do know—at some point Gehazi had to be brought before the king. Otherwise, how could he wind up there? When the king's messengers would have brought Gehazi before the king, the king could have repeated his inquiry. "Now how did this happen?" The now exhilarated Gehazi began to tell his amazing story of miraculous restoration . . .

Can you imagine the scene in the king's court that day? In the beginning, soldiers, courtiers, and king all kept their distance from the leper who now claimed to be clean—*just in case.* As the story unfolded in incredible detail after detail, the heads of Gehazi's hearers must have bobbed back and forth between the king and the former leper's baby-smooth face like spectators at a modern tennis match.

By the end of the story, everyone wanted to grab the man's restored hand.

Ancient kings from many different cultures and empires often offered magnificent rewards or very prominent positions of power to honored individuals who had saved their lives, served their nations, or performed acts of outstanding bravery on behalf of the throne. It would not be unlike a king in those days to say:[8]

"How may I reward you? What may be done to honor the fact that you and your sons risked your lives to enter the Syrian army encampment, and then returned to share your discovery of food and supplies with our starving city? What may be done for the bringer of good news?"

As he observed Gehazi's humility in response, even the king wondered if he had found an arm upon which he would be happy to lean. King Jehoram of Samaria, Israel, wondered what he could do for Gehazi. He settled on a brilliant solution that would solve two pressing problems in one stroke.

A Sudden Job Opening Due to an Unfortunate Accident

He just happened to have a very sudden job opening due to the unfortunate accident at the main gate earlier—he was in serious need of "one upon whose arm the king could lean," a confidant to replace the one run over by good news.

"Gehazi, I have a sudden job opening that would be perfect for you. Yes, this is the answer. *Scribe—write this down.*

"Concerning the former leper, Gehazi, Jehoram the King of Samaria, Israel, hereby rewards you with a special title and position of importance.

"You shall spend the rest of your days in the king's court, serving my royal presence.

"Therefore, the king decrees that you and your family shall be cared for and provided with a royal allowance, including garments, silver, and any other need for the rest of your lives. All of your needs shall be met according to the king's riches and glory, henceforth and forever."

> **Somebody's coming back— make sure it's you!**

Suddenly, Gehazi is back! Not just in health, but also in position!

Somebody is coming back. The arrogant man that Gehazi replaced made mistakes that led to his demise. You sure don't want to make those kinds of mistakes. The king's official *heard* good news, but because he rejected what he should have accepted, he got run over by "good news," and he never made it back. Avoid those mistakes, and make the same right decisions Gehazi made, because somehow they brought him all the way back. He stepped right into the vacuum made by the other man who *didn't* come back.

Somebody's coming back—make sure it's *you*!

This may be a fictional dialogue about a biblical event that took place thousands of years ago, but it can also represent a picture of God's blessing in your life! If you do what is pleasing to the King, He will see to it that your needs are supplied! You too can be in His presence in the King's court.

CHAPTER 12

Guess Who Came Back With Him?
Restoration Can Be Contagious

One stroke of God's favor seemed to erase seven years of unspeakable pain. Imagine Gehazi in the king's court, talking, serving, and looking as if he had never suffered ill.

How could we bridge the gap and dream up a promotion like this one for Gehazi? It is part of the process of filling in the gap between what we *know* happened and what *may* have happened. The last time we heard about Gehazi *by name*, he had just been struck with full-blown leprosy.

Then we see Jehoram, king of Israel, leaning on Gehazi's arm. This was, possibly, Gehazi's first day on the job as the one "on whose hand the king leaned."

Then the king leans closer to ask Gehazi, "Now where did you formerly work?"

"I used to serve the great prophet Elisha."

"Oh, yes! I *know* about him. Are all of those stories true? Tell me a story about Elisha."

"Well, let's see, okay, one time Elisha met a childless Shunammite woman who had her husband prepare a prophet's quarters just for Elisha's use.

"At my suggestion, he prayed for the woman and while doing so prophesied that she would have a son. That son was born exactly as

Elisha predicted, and all went well until several years later when the boy suddenly collapsed while in the fields with his father and later died on his mother's knees.

"The Shunammite woman placed her son's lifeless body on the prophet's bed and then raced to find Elisha. He and I were on Mount Carmel. The prophet sent me ahead with instructions to lay his staff on the body of the dead child, but it did no good.

"Finally Elisha arrived, entered the room with the body, and locked the door behind him. After he prayed over the boy, we heard sounds of pacing and then we heard someone sneeze seven times. The next thing I knew, Elisha was telling me, 'Call this Shunammite woman.' Then all he said to her was, 'Pick up your son.' Her dead son had been raised back to life!"[1]

Then the king looked up, and he suddenly raised a hand to catch Gehazi's attention and said, "Hold on, Gehazi. That's a great story—but you'll have to finish it later. I need to hear the next case scheduled to be brought before me. It's about an eviction notice."[2]

Gehazi abruptly ended his story and looked up, only to blurt out, "My lord, O king, this is the woman, and this is her son, whom Elisha restored to life."[3]

An Epiphany!

It was at this place in the biblical narrative that the connection suddenly became clear to me. The Gehazi of the story seven years ago and the Gehazi upon whom the king leaned was one and the same person. *How else would he recognize the woman?*

Once again, let me reemphasize the fact that I don't know **how** all of this *really* happened. No one on earth really knows these things. The details of Gehazi's miraculous transformation and restoration from life as a condemned and despised leper to the position of personal assistant to the king of Israel are unknown. It's a secret we can only speculate about. The process is unknown, but the outcome is known.

Musing Over Educated Guesses and Studied Suppositions

The actual steps Gehazi took from "here" to "there" are shrouded in mystery. Only God Himself knows the facts about Gehazi's rise from his miserable life as a leper to chief official in the inner courts of the king.

What I have shared so far are educated guesses and studied suppositions from personal research and thoughts of some leading Christian and Jewish scholars and theologians.

We don't know how or when the restoration came, but *we know it did happen.* Only God could have or would have done such a thing.

In one chapter Gehazi and his sons were hopelessly trapped in the hell of leprosy. A few chapters later he shows up apparently free of his fatal disease, restored to high position, and retelling the story of his former master's miracle with the woman and her son.

Perhaps you face what appears to be a hopeless future. You are positive that God can deliver you, but you keep trying to figure out how He is going to do it. Stop!

Stop Trying to Figure God Out!

You are thinking, *It's going to come this way,* or *It will happen that way,* but a totally unexpected restorative process may be sneaking in the back door of your life.

Just a side note to the critics and naysayers in your life—warn them it would be wise to avoid doorways, gates, and other pathways or thoroughfares that your promise may be coming through!

It can be dangerous to stand in a doorway of promise created by prophetic obedience! When God opens the windows of heaven, good news is on its way!

Some belief-challenged folks have been known to get run over by good news!

Within the course of a single day, Gehazi's name gained the power to open doors. Only twenty-four hours earlier, his name closed every door he encountered—including the city gate. Any mention of his name in polite company brought disparaging remarks, sneers, and social bankruptcy.

There was no place for Gehazi to reenter the social structure of his family or the marketplace of business, much less the court of the king. But that's still not all—there is more good news coming!

When the ultimate comeback turned Gehazi's life around, guess who came back with him? You should know that restoration can be contagious!

Restoration Can Be Contagious!

Those who love and care about you are linked to the consequences of your actions for good or for evil. They are blessed when you are blessed and, unfortunately, they are cursed when you are cursed. The first in line are often the members of your own family.

We see it every year: Headlines trumpet the stories by the dozens in newspapers, magazines, and TV documentaries:

- "CEO Convicted of Securities Fraud, Tax Evasion"
- "Properties Confiscated"
- "Funds Seized"
- "Retirement Revoked"
- "Penalties Levied"
- "Jail Time Possible!"

Very few seem to mourn over people convicted of such crimes, but what about the innocent spouses, sons, and daughters who may know almost nothing about the day-to-day activities of their guilty family members?

The people related to convicted power brokers from Wall Street, the Pentagon, Silicon Valley, or Capitol Hill probably knew very little about the illegal decisions made in boardrooms, bedrooms, or the CEO's office. It doesn't matter—they are doomed to share the consequences together.

The innocent spouse and children are often dragged through hell when infidelity ruins a marriage. What about the parents of someone addicted to drugs? How do you think they feel? They are condemned to walk through the hell of addiction through no fault of their own! How painful can that be? Perhaps you can relate to this?

Regardless of whether the negative consequences came through your actions, or if you are the innocent one believing for restoration, I have more good news!

If you live in painful regret over the way your mistakes have impacted others in your life, step into Gehazi's shoes for just a moment—immediately *after* his ultimate comeback.

Restoration can be contagious!

Think of the emotional waterfall experienced by Gehazi's family the night he showed up at the door with his sons! The sorrow and stigma of seven long, painful years spent in constant worry about the future evaporated in an instant!

Imagine the impact Gehazi's miracle restoration had on the Gehazi family financial portfolio: After nearly seven years without his income or his presence in the home as father and husband, Gehazi's family suddenly enjoyed the full financial favor of the king of Israel!

No longer would Mrs. Gehazi be forced to sneak out to public markets at odd times to avoid the rejection inevitable for families of lepers and outcasts. Never again would they be forced to submit to the hundreds of small injustices and private insults they had endured as a "condemned family" living under the shadow of a public curse.

After seven years of sharing the weight and pain of her husband's nationally publicized curse, now Mrs. Gehazi and her family were beginning to enjoy the fruits and benefits of Gehazi's incredible restoration.

"Plan Your Weddings, Girls! Daddy's Home!"

Once Gehazi experienced his miraculous comeback, any daughters he had could go forward with plans to finalize marriages. "*Plan your weddings, girls! Daddy's home!*" (Before Gehazi's miracle turnaround, any marriage plans would have been placed on permanent hold. Who would want to marry into a family of lepers?)

Gehazi's name was restored to the spiritual archives of honor after seven years of desecration as the poster boy of criminal and selfish betrayal of prophetic trust. Restoration truly *is* contagious—*when Gehazi rose again, so did his battered family.*

> **When you "come back," your family can "come back" with you!**

His sons—public victims of their father's private sins for seven years— were now restored overnight to health and positive public standing. They became instant heroes because of their father's public heroism and righteous choices.

Before that night, no one in Samaria would have wanted to associate with Gehazi's family, not only because of the religious and social stigma, but also because of the sheer fear of contracting a frightening contagious disease.

Suddenly, everyone wants Gehazi and his family over for dinner. His wife is asked to be key speaker at the local Samarian Women's Auxiliary, and Gehazi probably hired a social secretary just to manage his exploding social appointment calendar. Churches wanted to hear his testimony!

Gehazi's Overnight Transformation Should Give You Hope

Religious leaders would remember Gehazi's betrayal for centuries, and many would claim he was never worthy of restoration. "He betrayed the Man of God." But his comeback is real, even though it's impossible to fully explain.

If you are feeling broken and discouraged like a discarded failure, then Gehazi's *overnight transformation* from lowly leper to intimate friend and confidant of the king should give you hope.

God gave Gehazi a miracle turnaround that blessed his entire family.

Are you ready for a "comeback spirit" to enter your life? Even if you've managed to mangle "Plan A" for your life, God has a great "Plan B" for you too! He can make Romans 8:28 come true in your life. "And we know that all things work together for good to them that love God . . ."[4]

Let praise to God enter your life—no matter how dark and impossible it may be at the moment. Allow El Shaddai, "the God of More Than Enough"—to begin filling your empty spaces.[5]

Exchange the Bitterness of Your Life for the Joy of the Lord

It doesn't matter how far gone you think you are! God allows U-turns! Stop making bad decisions. Start making good decisions. You are coming back!

Exchange your heartbreak for His wholeness! Trade your lack for His plenty! Give Him the weight of your bitter pain and rise up in His joy!

One thing should stand out above all your efforts to survive and beyond all your fears, pain, and suffering. God loves you. Let me say it again, God *really* loves you.

Recently I picked up my thirteen-year-old daughter from school and when I asked, "How you doing, big girl?" she just sighed and said, "Had a bad day, Dad." Then she went into all the things that had happened.

As I reached over to hug her, I said, "That's seventh graders for you. That's just how people act; that's how they are sometimes." I hadn't cheered her up much, because she was still stuck in the moment. It was time for the Final Option, the offer of last resort in times of crisis.

"Are you hungry?"

"Yeah, I'm a little bit hungry."

Swallowing hard, I said, "You want to go to McDonald's?"

She looked at me like I'd grown a third eye square in the middle of my furrowed forehead. The look on her face basically said, *It's a miracle—it's a real miracle!*

"You will actually take me to McDonald's?"

"Well, I didn't say I would *eat* there with you, but I'll *take* you." (No offense meant, but I don't like any fast food, especially McDonald's.

When I have to go there, I claim the Scripture that says, "If you eat any deadly thing . . .")

"You would do that for me, Daddy?"

It Wasn't the Food, It Was My Love for My Daughter

I didn't care for the food, but I loved my daughter! I didn't know what she needed, but *I was willing to go somewhere I didn't want to go and do something I didn't necessarily want to do* just to reach out to her and help supply what she needed!

(I seem to remember Someone else who went somewhere He didn't want to go and willingly did something He did not want to do—Jesus supplied what we *all* needed but could not acquire on our own!⁶)

In fact, Jesus supplied everything *you* need for a *comeback* from fear, failure, despair, and death. The next step is up to *you*. The first step in your restoration is just that—you need to take the first step. Make the first move *now*.

Start marching toward God's promises—even if you feel you can barely hobble through a life crippled by mistakes, missteps, and evil circumstances. Health can be yours!

Step out of the shadows of your failures and fears. Start your journey with a step of obedience, and follow that with praise and worship so God can launch a "comeback miracle" in your life!

The gap between Plan A and Plan B in Gehazi's life is so incredible that we don't even know for sure how God brought the man back into the biblical record!

If "Plan A" was working for the prophet, then "Plan B" is being in the king's court! Is it possible that God can make Plan B better than Plan A?

The good news is that *the end result is more important than the journey* in your life. Your life isn't too far gone. When you are down to nothing, God is up to something!

No matter how seriously you've failed God or man, *the God who sees the end before the beginning* has a miraculous Plan B in store for you.

If loved ones in your life seem to be too distant, do what the Shunammite mother in Elisha's day did—lay them on the bed of God's promises and run for His presence! Jesus prayed for Peter and he *came back*! Who are you praying for? (Remember: Restoration can be contagious!)

Your hidden places desperately need God's restoration power. Take courage. When you are restored, you will bring restoration to others!

God uses ordinary people like you and me. He insists on using an army of unlikely heroes so that everyone *knows* it is God's doing, not ours!

There is restoration even for the most improbable! Let Gehazi be your guide. Let Samson be your signpost.

It isn't too late for you—you are a candidate for the ultimate comeback!

Stop putting yourself down. Look up and step out. A turnaround is coming!

"Can you tell me how God is going to do it?"

"No."

"Can God really do all that?"

"And more."

"How is He going to do it?"

"I don't know. I just know He can!"

Believe and begin your ultimate comeback right now.

I would love to hear from you.
Let me hear how this book inspired your own personal comeback.
Please visit www.godchasers.net/ultimatecomeback
and share your story with me.

Tony Tony

The Ultimate Comeback Road

1: Realize the tomb of failure can become the womb of success.

2: Stop looking at the past. Never, ever let your past dictate your future.

3: Develop a "nothing to lose" mentality.

4: Lay down your life in His presence so He can impart His life.

5: Obedience is God's excuse to bless you.

6: Pass the test when it comes around again.

7: Never quit. You cannot lose if you do not quit.

Notes

Chapter 1: You're Fired!

1. Job 1:1 (NKJV).
2. See Matthew 5:45.
3. John 11:44 (NKJV, emphasis mine).
4. John 11:43b (NIV, emphasis mine).
5. John 10:10b (NKJV).
6. Hebrews 11:32–33 (NKJV, emphasis mine).
7. Galatians 6:7b (NKJV).
8. I don't know how long Samson was forced to work as a human donkey, grinding corn at the mill for man's amusement, but it had to be longer than merely eight or ten weeks. It was most likely at least a year long.

Chapter 2: The Tale of the Almond Tree

1. See Psalm 23:4.
2. Numbers 17:1–4 (KJV, emphasis mine).
3. Numbers 17:4 (KJV).
4. See Romans 3:23.

Chapter 3: I Feel Stripped, Bare, and Dry

1. Numbers 17:4 (KJV, emphasis mine).
2. Numbers 17:7–8 (KJV, emphasis mine).

3. "But, beloved, be not ignorant of this one thing, that one day is with the Lord as a thousand years, and a thousand years as one day" (2 Peter 3:8 KJV).

4. Isaiah 40:31 says, "But they that wait upon the LORD shall renew their strength; they shall mount up with wings as eagles; they shall run, and not be weary; and they shall walk, and not faint" (KJV).

5. See 2 Timothy 4:7–8.

6. Numbers 17:9–10 (NKJV, emphasis mine).

7. Hebrews 9:4 (NKJV, emphasis mine).

8. See Exodus 16:19–20.

9. Exodus 16:33–34 (NKJV, emphasis mine).

10. James Strong, *Strong's Exhaustive Concordance of the Bible* (Peabody, MA: Hendrickson Publishers, n.d.), Hebrew #4931. mishmereth, fem. Of H4929; watch, i.e., the act (custody) or (concr.) *the sentry*, the *post*; obj. *preservation*, or (concr.) safe; fig. observance, i.e. (abstr.) duty, or (obj.) a usage or party.—charge, keep, to be kept, office, ordinance, safeguard, ward, watch. [Italics mine.]

11. Acts 19:13–17 (NKJV).

12. Proverbs 18:10 (NKJV).

13. See John 4:23–24.

14. See Matthew 17:16; Mark 9:18; Luke 9:40.

15. The very first statement in the Westminster Short Catechism says, "What is the chief end of man? Man's chief end is to glorify God, and to enjoy him forever." (This catechism or short summary of doctrine is used by English-speaking Presbyterians as well as some Congregationalist and Baptist congregations.) Source: www.reformed.org/doc uments/WSC.html.

16. For instance, in Colossians 4:11 (NIV), Paul lists "Jesus, who is called Justus," as one of his fellow workers in the gospel.

Chapter 4: The "Oops" Chapter of Life

1. 2 Kings 5:1 (NKJV, emphasis mine).

2. Cancer is *not* contagious—we just treat its victims as if it is.

3. 2 Kings 5:3b (NKJV).

4. See 2 Kings 5:4–5.

5. See 2 Kings 5:6–8 (NKJV).

6. 2 Kings 5:9 (NKJV).

7. 2 Kings 5:10 (NKJV).

8. 2 Kings 5:11–12 (NKJV).

9. See John 14:15 (a command for *all* of us), and Luke 18:22 (a very personal command or "spiritual prescription" *not* specifically required of anyone else in the Gospels except for "the rich young ruler," whose life was built on a false foundation of worldly wealth).

10. See what happened to Saul in 1 Samuel 15.

11. 2 Kings 5:13b (NKJV).

12. See John 9:6–7 and Mark 7:32–37 for examples of the Lord's unusual ministry methods.

13. 2 Kings 5:14 (NKJV).

14. 2 Kings 5:16 (NKJV).

15. See 2 Kings 5:17.

16. 2 Kings 5:20 (NKJV).

17. 2 Kings 5:21b (KJV).

18. 2 Kings 5:22a (KJV, emphasis mine).

19. *The New Living Translation* equates a talent of silver with approximately 75 pounds of the precious metal. At an arbitrary rate of $7.55 per troy ounce (there are 12 troy ounces to the pound), 75 pounds of silver was equal to approximately $6,795 as of this writing. Two talents of silver would equal approximately $13,590—a great fortune by the standards of antiquity.

20. 2 Kings 5:24 (KJV, emphasis mine).

21. *Strong's Exhaustive Concordance of the Bible*, Hebrew #6076. 'ophel, o'-fel; *from H6075*; a turior; also a mound, i.e. fortress:—emerod, fort, strong hold, tower. **6075**. 'aphal, aw-fal'; a prim. root; to swell; fig. be elated:—**be lifted up, presume**.

22. 2 Kings 5:25 (KJV).

23. 2 Kings 5:26 (NKJV).

24. 2 Kings 5:27 (NKJV).

25. 2 Kings 5:26b (KJV, emphasis mine).

26. 2 Kings 5:27a (KJV, emphasis mine).

Chapter 5: This Could Be a Miserable Year

1. 2 Kings 5:27a (NKJV, emphasis mine).

2. See Joshua 7 for the full story of Achan, the man who brought a curse on his entire nation and a death sentence on his family by gathering gold, silver, and garments that God said were accursed.

3. See 2 Kings 5:25–27.

4. Luke 10:18 (NKJV, emphasis mine).

5. Isaiah 14:12-15, 24 (NKJV, emphasis mine).

6. See 2 Kings 2:1-16; 3:4–34; 4:8–17, 18–37; 6:18–23.

7. Leviticus 13:45–46 (NASB).

8. Some scholars argue that leprosy in the Old Testament was more a problem of divine judgment for violation of religious ritual than an actual physical disease like the leprosy we know today as "Hansen's disease." (Everybody *does* seem to agree that it was a terrible condition with bad consequences.) I am convinced that leprosy in Gehazi's day was *more* than just a ritually unclean condition. (Why else would a Syrian get it?)

9. Numbers 12:12–13 (NASB, emphasis mine).

10. Centers for Disease Control (CDC), Division of Bacterial and Mycotic Disease (DBMD), "Hansen's Disease (Leprosy)—Technical Information" posting says 763,917 new cases of leprosy were detected worldwide in 2002, with 96 cases showing up in the United States.

    Two forms of Hansen's are described, the weaker form being limited to patchy skin areas that were neither raised nor lower than the surrounding skin tissue, and lacking the normal skin pigmentation found elsewhere.

    The serious form, Multibacillary Hansen's disease, is associated with "symmetric skin lesions, nodules, plaques, thickened dermis, and frequent involvement of the nasal mucosa resulting in nasal congestion and epistaxis (recurring bleeding from the nose)."

    The bacillus, *Mycobacterium leprae*, affects the skin, nerves, and mucous membranes. About 2 million people are permanently disabled at this time as a result of Hansen's disease.

    The same report claims that "persons receiving antibiotic treatment or having complete treatment are considered free of active infection."

In the very next paragraph, the CDC admits that the medical world is uncertain about how this disease is transmitted (accessed via the Internet at *http://www.cdc.gov/ncidod/dbmd/diseaseinfo/hansens_t.htm*).

In other more recent scientific postings by the World Health Organization and the CDC, leprosy appears to be making major advances in Third World nations where the disease seems totally immune from attempts to create vaccines or treat the disease.

11. The Levitical instructions given through Moses actually said that once a person was *completely covered* with white scales, then *that person was ritually clean* and could be readmitted to the congregation of God after appropriate ritual cleansing (see Leviticus 13:12-13). Obviously, this was *not* the case with Gehazi! He may have been as white as snow, but the Bible clearly says he was leprous. Therefore, he must have also manifested the "raw flesh" within the white encrustations (see Leviticus 13:14–15). The prophet was in no mood to dispense a light slap on his deceitful servant's hand, and Gehazi didn't respond like someone who had just been pardoned from a death sentence. He disappeared from the Bible record for as many as seven years before reappearing in the close company of the king of Israel. The king was an observant Jew who would want *no close physical contact* with a leper or even a former leper as famous as Gehazi—unless he had been totally healed.

12. *Strong's Exhaustive Concordance of the Bible*, Hebrew #1522, *Gechazi*, valley of a visionary; and #6879, *tsara*, a prim. root; to scourge, i.e., (intrans. and fig.) to be stricken with leprosy.

13. See 2 Kings 6:32.

14. I'm thinking of the Jewish picture of Gehenna—in the Hebrew, *Ge-Hinnom*, in the Greek, *gehenna*. Merrill F. Unger, *Unger's Bible Dictionary*, 3rd ed. (Chicago: Moody Bible Institute of Chicago, 1987), under the article, "Gehenna"; pp. 394–95.

15. The story appears in many places, but details have been excerpted from *Theology Today*, vol. 40, no. 2, July 1983, "Gandhi: The Person and the Film," by Susanna Oommen Younger, an East Indian and a graduate of Madras and Kerala Universities, and Princeton Theological

Seminary, who now lives in Dundas, Ontario. Accessed via the Internet at *http://theologytoday.ptsem.edu/jul1983/v40-2-article5.htm*.

Chapter 6: The Ultimate Comeback!

1. 2 Kings 8:3–4 (NKJV, emphasis mine).
2. Please understand that our humor in this passage is directly solely toward Gehazi, whose own actions placed himself in the predicament of battling leprosy. Even so, we would not indulge in such humor if Gehazi's own story had not turned around so miraculously in God's Word. In no way do we wish to express humor at the expense of those battling the very real health problems posed today by Hansen's disease, or any other wasting disease with similar symptoms.
3. See Romans 11:25; Ephesians 5:32; 1 Timothy 3:16.
4. Isaiah 46:9b–10a (NKJV, emphasis mine).
5. 2 Kings 8:5a (NLT).
6. See Mark 10:13–15; John 12:20–22.
7. See 2 Kings 4:29.
8. See 2 Kings 4:36–37.
9. 2 Kings 8:1–6 (NLT, emphasis mine).
10. See 2 Kings 15:1–5.

Chapter 7: God Does His Best Work in Secret

1. 2 Kings 5:27 (*The Message*, emphasis mine).
2. Esther 6:1a (KJV, emphasis mine). Experience the life-changing revelation of Esther's miraculous and prophetic life and how it applies to *you* today by reading my two best-selling books, *Finding Favor with the King* (a nonfiction work revealing the detailed revelation of the power of intimacy in the presence of the King of kings) and *Hadassah: One Night With the King,* a national best-selling fiction novel based on this revelation of the life of Esther. Both books are available at your local Christian bookstore or through our ministry, GodChasers.Network at *www.godchasers.net*.
3. Esther 6:1a (KJV). Again, read *Finding Favor with the King* if you want to capture the full power, drama, and anointing of God that permeates this much misunderstood book of the Bible.

4. See Esther 5:9–14.

5. See Esther 6:1–4.

6. Esther 6:1 (KJV).

7. See Esther 2:21–23.

8. See Esther 6:3–11 (KJV).

9. Psalm 121:4 (KJV).

10. Psalm 30:5b (KJV).

11. Esther 6:6 (NKJV).

12. See Esther 6:8 (KJV).

13. Esther 6:9 (NKJV, emphasis mine).

14. See *Finding Favor with the King* for the "rest of the story" behind Esther's astounding rescue of her people, and of Haman's bitter end.

15. Esther 7:3–4 (NKJV).

16. Esther 7:5b (NKJV).

17. Esther 7:6 (NKJV).

18. See Esther 7:8b (NKJV).

19. Esther 8:1-2 (KJV, emphasis mine).

20. Deuteronomy 29:29 (NKJV, emphasis mine).

21. Esther 8:17b (KJV, emphasis mine).

22. See Judges 16:19–21.

23. See Judges 16:26 (NKJV).

24. Philippians 1:21 (NKJV).

25. Judges 16:28b (NKJV).

26. Judges 16:30 (*The Message*).

27. If all of this sounds too "warlike" for Christian people, I invite you to consider the "reason the Son of God appeared" according to John: It was to "*destroy* the works of the devil" (1 John 3:8 NKJV, emphasis mine). We are called to follow in His footsteps. We cannot duplicate His atoning death on the cross, but we *are* expected to do the works He did "and greater" (see John 14:12). However, we do not battle against *people* because our enemies are not "flesh and blood." Paul said we battle against spiritual foes and opponents in the heavenlies (see Ephesians 6:12).

28. John 11:43 (NKJV).

29. A *"rhema"* is a specific and personal "now" word of revelation from God. Jesus Christ was the *Logos*, the living embodiment of God's Word, the "Word made flesh," the "Divine Expression" of God. When the two are one, mountains move, the sick are healed, and the dead rise.
30. See Acts 13:13.
31. See Luke 9:62.
32. Acts 15:37–41 (*The Message*).
33. 2 Timothy 4:9–11 (*The Message*, emphasis mine). Second Timothy 4:11 in the KJV reads: ". . . he is profitable to me for the ministry."
34. See Matthew 27:45–54; Mark 15:33; and Luke 23:44–48. Darkness covered Jerusalem *from noon until three o'clock* in the Lord's final hours before He died on the cross. Three hours of darkness on the cross, three days in the tomb, and then the Resurrection on the third day!

Chapter 8: Uh-Oh, I've Got a Bad Feeling About This

1. See 2 Kings 5:21, 25.
2. See 2 Kings 8:4–5.
3. 2 Kings 7:3 describes "four leprous men" at the city gate, and verse 8 describes "these lepers" when they enter the abandoned Syrian camp. A final mention appears in 2 Kings 15:5 describing how King Jotham was struck with leprosy.
4. 2 Kings 7:3–4a (NKJV).
5. 2 Kings 8:1b (NLT, emphasis mine).
6. See 2 Kings 6:25 (NLT).
7. 2 Kings 6:28–29 (*The Message*).
8. 2 Kings 7:3–4 (*The Message*, emphasis mine).
9. Luke 9:24 (NKJV).
10. Philippians 1:21 (NKJV).
11. 2 Kings 7:4b–7 (*The Message*).
12. 2 Corinthians 12:10b (NKJV).
13. See Judges 8:10, which shows 120,000 fell in the initial battle (mostly as Gideon's opponents attacked one another, and 15,000 were caught and killed later with their leaders).

14. See Revelation 1:18.
15. 2 Kings 7:8 (*The Message*).
16. See 2 Kings 7:9b (KJV).

Chapter 9: I've Got Good News and I've Got Bad News

1. 2 Kings 7:8b–9 (*The Message*, emphasis mine).
2. Leviticus 13:45–46 (KJV, emphasis mine).
3. *JewishEncyclopedia.com*, article by Emil G. Hirsch (citing Sotah 47a). www.comeandhear.com/sotah/sotah_47.html.
4. See 2 Kings 5:23.
5. *JewishEncyclopedia.com*, Hirsch.
6. See Luke 22:31–34.
7. See Matthew 26:69–75; Luke 22:54–63.
8. See John 21:14–18.
9. See John 21:18–19.

Chapter 10: I'm Going Back

1. 2 Kings 7:9 (NKJV, emphasis mine).
2. We know this from the serious treatment leprosy receives in the writings of Moses, and especially since God used the disease in the Old Testament to bring correction. While I'm convinced He does not do this under the New Covenant, it is arguable that all He did with Miriam, Moses's sister, and Gehazi was *reveal in the natural or physical realm* what kind of *spiritual disease* was actually at work in human hearts. Paul did something similar when dealing with a case of incest in the Corinthian church, telling them: "To deliver such an one unto Satan for the destruction of the flesh, that the spirit may be saved in the day of the Lord Jesus" (1 Corinthians 5:5 KJV). It seems the man *did* repent and Paul had to encourage the same church to forgive him and allow him to start over (see 2 Corinthians 2:6–9).
3. See 2 Kings 5:23–27.
4. We should note that Gehazi and his sons *did* have some positive motivation to do the right thing. All four men had family members who were left behind when leprosy separated them from their family and all forms of polite society.

5. Luke 17:11–14 (NKJV, emphasis mine). It is especially interesting to me that the Bible specifically notes that the *one* leper who returned to thank Jesus for being cleansed was a *Samaritan* who was healed in Samaria.

6. 2 Kings 7:9–11 (NKJV, emphasis mine).

7. See John 4:28–30 (NLT, emphasis mine).

8. 2 Kings 7:9 (NKJV, emphasis mine).

9. 2 Kings 7:12 (NKJV, emphasis mine).

Chapter 11: Run Over By Good News!

1. 2 Kings 7:1 (NLT, emphasis mine).

2. 2 Kings 7:2 (KJV, emphasis mine).

3. Ibid.

4. See 2 Kings 7:13.

5. 2 Kings 7:2 (NLT, emphasis mine).

6. 2 Kings 7:12 (NKJV).

7. Based on the priestly instructions in Leviticus 13 and 14, the men could be examined and quarantined for seven to fourteen days, and then would return on the eighth day so the priest could offer sacrifices to pronounce them ceremonially clean.

8. We often see the practice in the Scriptures. For example: Daniel was promoted to second place under the king of the Babylonian Empire, and later under the Persian kings Darius and Cyrus; David was promoted to captain of Israel's armies by Saul, and to the office of king and prophet over Judah and Israel by God; Joseph was promoted to second-in-command under Egypt's pharaoh; and Esther's cousin, Mordecai the Jew, was promoted to second in power under King Xerxes of Persia.

Chapter 12: Guess Who Came Back With Him?

1. Adapted from the narrative in 2 Kings 4:8–37 and 8:1–5.

2. See 2 Kings 8:3–5.

3. 2 Kings 8:5b (KJV).

4. KJV.

5. See Genesis 17:1 where God first revealed Himself to Abram as the "Almighty God" (*El Shaddai* is the Hebrew transliteration of the term).

6. See John 3:16.

RUN WITH US

I would love to connect with you.

As a GodChasers.network Ministry partner you will receive . . .

❖ A TEACHING CD EVERY MONTH
(featuring recent messages from Tommy Tenney)

❖ A SPECIAL LETTER EVERY MONTH FROM ME TO YOU

❖ 25% OFF ANY PRODUCT FROM GODCHASERS.NETWORK

The ministry I do around the world couldn't happen without people partnering with me. *I* need you, and *they* need God — be the link that brings us together.

Become a GodChasers.network Ministry Partner today . . .

Online at:
www.godchasers.net
click "Ministry Partner" located on the side menu

By mail:
P.O. Box 3355
Pineville, LA 71361
write "Ministry Partner Sign-up" in the memo line of your check

By phone:
(318) 442-4273

JOIN THE CHASE!

WHAT YOU CAN DO AT www.godchasers.net:

✓ Order products from our online store
✓ Check Upcoming Events
✓ Sign-up for Daily Devotions by email or text message
✓ Sign-up for Tommy Tenney teachings by PODcast or MP3 Downloads
✓ Sign-up to be a Ministry Partner or a Prayer Partner

GodChasers.network   P.O. Box 3355 Pineville, LA 71361, USA   (318) 442-4273

GODCHASERS
INTERNATIONAL
MINISTRY SCHOOL
. . . PASSIONATELY PURSUING THE PRESENCE OF GOD

Are you hungry for hands-on training from leaders who are passionate about discipleship? Are you passionate about His presence? If so, this is the school for you.

Our program offers a variety of experiences with five tracks of ministry to choose from:
Worship · Pastoral · Youth · Children · Mission Ministries

We offer advanced training through personal mentoring with a Bible-based foundation. God Chasers student life hosts numerous events during the semester to bring students, faculty, and staff together.

WHAT YOU CAN EXPECT FROM
THE GODCHASERS INTERNATIONAL MINISTRY SCHOOL:

1. Mentoring Environment
2. Practical Hands-on Ministry
3. Solid Biblical Foundation
4. Opportunity to Minister in Corporate Settings
5. Equipping Passionate Worshippers
6. Spiritual Training Ground That Releases the Gifts of the Spirit
7. Equipping That Will Launch You into Your Future
8. A Place of Destiny and Excitement

VISIT OUR WEBSITE TO FIND OUT MORE: www.godchasers.net/ministryschool

Our vision is to leave a spiritual legacy of passionate young men and women. We want to fuel their passion and impart to them the lessons we have learned. "My deepest desire is to launch the next generation of GodChasers and see them passionately pursuing God's presence."

–Tommy and Jeannie Tenney
GodChasers.network

GodChasers Ministry School is calling to those who will lay down their lives and pick up their mantle. Our mandate is to reach the earth with the gospel. Our deep passion for Jesus will bring that to pass.

–Keith and Darla Collins
GCIMS President/Administrator

WHAT ARE YOU WAITING FOR? LAUNCH INTO YOUR DESTINY!

P.O. BOX 3355
PINEVILLE, LA 71361 USA
PH: (318) 442-4273 ~ FAX: (318) 487-6856
Email: admissionsinfo@godchasers.net, web: www.godchasers.net/ministryschool

Would you like to receive a daily encouraging word from Tommy Tenney?

Sign up to receive Daily Devotions straight to your inbox.

Devotions are based on the bestselling books you love and the thought provoking sermons you have listened to. Join up and allow readable revelations to infiltrate your life, one day at a time.

Sign up today and be among the first to read inspiring insights from Tommy's newest book

THE ULTIMATE COMEBACK

Sign up online at:
www.godchasers.net

~select the "Daily Devotional" button on the side menu~

OR

Sign up for two-line text message devotions for your cell phone.

~visit *www.godchasers.net* for instructions on how you can receive short and sweet inspirational words that pack a punch~
Standard messaging, data, and other rates may apply